Understanding History

and other Essays

UNDERSTANDING HISTORY

HISTORY

And Other Essays

by

BERTRAND RUSSELL

PHILOSOPHICAL LIBRARY

New York

Contents

How to Read and Understand History . . . 9

The Value of Free Thought 57

Mentalism vs. Materialism 105

   The Meaning of Matter 106

   The Nature of "Mass" 106

   Ups and Downs of the Atomic Theory 107

   Quantum Theory 108

   The Behavior of Matter in Bulk 109

   Physics Is Still Deterministic 110

   Psychology Also Has Changed 111

   Life As It Appears in Biology 112

   What We Mean by Habit 113

   Habit Primarily Physical 114

   Physical Causes of Introspection 116

   The Physical and Mental Overlap 118

   Definition of "Physical" 118

   The Relations Between Mental and Physical Events 120

   The Question of "Materialism" 121

How to Read and Understand History

It is not of history as a subject of academic instruction that I wish to write. The newspapers say that the young do not know enough history when they leave school; the young, after cramming for examinations, feel that they know too much, and set to work to forget what they have learnt as soon as possible. In universities, professional historians give lectures of two kinds: survey courses, which are remembered only long enough to secure credits, and advanced courses for those who mean to spend their lives teaching history to people who will teach history to . . . All this is no doubt very valuable, but it is not the subject of this essay. My subject is history as a pleasure, as an agreeable and profitable way of spending such leisure as an exacting world may permit. I am not a professional historian, but I have read much history as an amateur. My purpose is to try to say what I have derived from history, and what many others, I am convinced, could derive without aiming at becoming specialists.

Now in the first place, if history is not necessary to your career, there is no point in reading it unless you enjoy it and find it interesting. I do not mean that the only point of history is to give pleasure—far from it. It has many other uses, which I shall try to explain in the course of this essay. But it will not have these uses except for those who enjoy it. The same is true of such things as music and painting and poetry. To study these things either because you must, or because you wish to be cultured, makes it almost impossible to acquire what they have to offer. Shakespeare wrote with a view to causing delight, and if you have any feeling for poetry he will delight you. But if he doesn't you had better let him alone. It is a dismal thing to inflict him upon school children until they hate the sound of his name; it is an insult to him and an injury to them. The *opportunity* to enjoy him should be offered to them, and will frequently be successful if it takes the shape of performing a play; but those to whom he is merely a bore should be allowed to occupy their time in some other way. History is not quite in the same case, because a modicum of history must be taught in schools. But whatever goes beyond this modicum should only be learnt by those who wish to know it, and even the modicum ought to be made as entertaining and pleasant as possible. Most children wish to know things until they go to school; in many cases it is bad teaching that makes them stupid and uninquiring.

There is history in the large and history in the small: each has its value, but their values are different. History in the large helps us to understand how the world developed into what it is; history in the small makes us know interesting men and women, and promotes a knowledge of human nature. Both should be learnt concurrently from the first. The method, in the early stages, should be largely by movies with explanatory talk.

History in the large answers (as far as may be) the question "how did things get here?" which is interesting to most intelligent children. It should begin with the sun throwing off planets, and should show the earth as a fiery ball, gradually cooling, with earthquakes, volcanoes, boiling seas and deluges of hot rain. Then gradually the various forms of life should be shown in the order of their appearance—forests of ferns, flowers and bees, odd fishes, vast reptiles fighting furious battles in the slime, awkward birds just learning to fly, mammals, small at first, but gradually growing bigger and more successful. Then comes early man—Pithecanthropus Erectus, the Piltdown man, the Neanderthal man, the Cro-Magnon man. He should be shown flying from wild beasts to the tops of trees, discovering fire and thereby acquiring safety in caves, escaping from sabre-toothed tigers into lake-dwellings, catching mammoths in pits, gradually perfecting his weapons and making himself, by intelligence, not strength, the Lord of Creation.

Then comes the beginning of civilization—agriculture in the Nile Valley and in Babylonia, the growth of the art of pottery, the evolution from stone to bronze, and thence, at last, to iron. At the same time could be shown the first civilized governments and religions—Egyptian kings and their pyramids and toiling slaves, mysterious dark temples lit up only once a year by the rising sun at the summer solstice, armies and the pomp of palaces. All this, in pictures, would delight almost any child, and would bring him, by easy stages, to the point where recorded history begins.

There is one aspect of history in the large in which there has been enormous increase in our knowledge during the last hundred years—I mean the history of the very earliest civilizations. This subject has a great deal of fascination, both in itself, and because of the detective ability that it calls for. The first great step was the deciphering of cuneiform, the writing of the Babylonians and Persians. Through tablets that have been excavated, a great deal is now known about the laws and customs and business methods of ancient Mesopotamia. Then there is the astonishing Minoan civilization of Crete, of which in classical Greece only a few legends survived. Unfortunately the Cretan script cannot, so far, be read, but from architecture and sculpture a great deal can be learnt. It seems that the Cretan upper classes were luxurious and rather decadent, fond of bull fights in which they employed female toreadors who performed the most astonishing acrobatic feats. It is only in modern times that nations have discovered how to be civilized without being decadent. The Cretans, rendered effeminate by luxury, appear to have been swept away by Greek pirates, who were then still barbarians. But for the victories of the Greeks over the Persians a millennium or more after the fall of Crete, Greek civilization might have disappeared as completely as that of the Minoan age.

The history of the development of arts and crafts, in its broad outlines, can be made interesting to very young children if it is presented in pictures with explanatory talk. The development of housing, of locomotion, of ships, and of agriculture is worth knowing something about before any detailed study of history begins; it gives a general sense of technical progress, slow at first, and then gradually more and more rapid, and it helps to form an imaginative picture of daily life in epochs very remote from our own. The part played by great rivers in the beginning of civilization is something which an intelligent child of six or seven years can understand. It is a mistake to begin education entirely from what is familiar; children have more free imagination than adults have, and they enjoy imaginative pictures of things very different from what they are used to. This is shown in the pleasure that almost all children find in playing Indian.

The later stages of history in the large are, in the main, less suitable for very young children than the earlier stages; probably, in most cases, they ought to wait until about the age of ten. It could then be explained that there have been three great ages of progress: the first, when agriculture was discovered, when kings became powerful and States began to grow, when vast buildings were erected in honor of kings and gods, when the art of writing was invented, the Babylonians discovered the rudiments of mathematics, and the arts of peace and war passed out of the barbarian stage. Next, after thousands of years of ossification, came the great age of Greece, from the time of Homer (whenever that was) to the death of Archimedes at the hands of a Roman soldier. Then another long period of decay and darkness, followed by the incredibly rapid progress from the 15th century to the present day. Throughout recorded history, progress has been the exception, not the rule; but when it has come, it has been swift and decisive.

Throughout this survey, certain important principles should emerge without being unduly emphasized. Periods of stagnation are those during which individuals feel powerless; periods of progress are those during which men feel that great achievements are possible, and that they wish to have their share. There has been in recent times a dangerous tendency, not unconnected with totalitarianism, to think only in terms of whole communities, and to ignore the contributions of individuals. But consider: some man or men invented the wheel, but in the American Continent it was unknown until the white men introduced it. Probably it was not one man who made the invention, but several men, starting from round logs used as rollers; however that may be, the difference that these men made to civilization is immeasurable. The need of individual genius is shown by the fact that the Mayas and the Incas, though in some ways highly civilized, never hit upon this simple invention. The difference between our world and the world before the industrial revolution is due to the discoveries and inventions of a small number of men; if, by some misfortune, a few thousand men of exceptional ability had perished in infancy, the technique of production would now be very little different from what it was in the 18th Century. Individuals can achieve great things, and the teacher of history ought to make this clear to his pupils. For without hope nothing of importance is accomplished.

History shows that the spread of civilization to new areas, as opposed to its intensification in a given region, has usually been due to military conquest. When a more civilized group conquers one which is less civilized, the conquered, if they are not too far beneath their conquerors, learn before long whatever their masters have to teach. But the converse also happens: when the conquerors are less civilized, if the war of conquest has not been too long or too destructive, they are apt to learn from their subjects. Greek civilization was diffused throughout the East by Alexander's victories, but throughout the West by the defeats inflicted on the Greeks by the Romans. Gaul and Spain were civilized by becoming subject to Rome; the Arabs, conversely, were civilized by conquering the Eastern portions of the Roman Empire. But although conquest has had a great effect in increasing the *area* of civilization, it has usually damaged its quality. Greece was less civilized after Alexander than before, and Rome was never as civilized as Greece had been.

Some of those who write history in the large are actuated by a desire to demonstrate some "philosophy" of history; they think they have discovered some formula according to which human events develop. The most notable are Hegel, Marx, Spengler, and the interpreters of the Great Pyramid and its "divine message." Various huge tomes (some of which I have possessed) have been written about the Great Pyramid, showing that it predicted the main outlines of history from the time when it was built to the date of publication of the tome in question. Soon after that date, there was to be fighting in Egypt, the Jews were to return to Palestine, and then there was to be the Second Coming and the end of the world. There has been fighting in Egypt, and the Jews are returning to Palestine, so the situation is alarming. However, there are still a good many Jews outside Palestine, so perhaps the message of the Great Pyramid is not for the immediate future.

Hegel's theory of history is not a whit less fantastic. According to him, there is something called "The Idea," which is always struggling to become the *Absolute* Idea. The Idea embodies itself first in one nation, then in another. It began with China, but finding it couldn't get very far there, it migrated to India. Then it tried the Greeks, and then the Romans. It was very pleased with Alexander and Caesar—it is noteworthy that it always prefers military men to intellectuals. But after Caesar it began to think there was nothing more to be done with the Romans, so after hesitating for four centuries or so it decided on the Germans, whom it has loved ever since, and still loved in the time of Hegel. However, their dominance is not to be eternal. The Idea always travels westward, and after leaving Germany it will migrate to America, where it will inspire a great war between the United States and Latin America. After that, if it continues to travel westward, I suppose it will reach Japan, but Hegel does not say so. When it has travelled round the world, the Absolute Idea will be realized, and mankind will be happy ever after. The Absolute Idea corresponds to the Second Coming.

It is odd that this fantastic theory—just as absurd, in its way, as the superstition about the Great Pyramid —should have been accepted as the acme of wisdom by innumerable professors, not only in Germany, where it appeals to national vanity, but in England and America, where it has no such adventitious advantage. What is still more surprising is that it underlies the doctrine of Marx, which is lauded by his disciples as the last word in all that is scientific. Marx made, it is true, a few changes: the "Idea" was replaced by the mode of production, the successive nations embodying the Idea were replaced by successive classes. But there was still the old mythological machinery. The Communist Revolution replaced the Second Coming, the dictatorship of the proletariat represented the rule of the saints, the Socialist Commonwealth was the emotional substitute for the millennium. Like the early Christians, Marx expected the millennium very soon; like their successors, his have been disappointed— once more, the world has shown itself recalcitrant to a tidy formula embodying the hopes of some section of mankind.

But not all general formulae professing to sum up

the course of past and future history are optimistic. Spengler has revived in our day the Stoics' doctrine of recurring cycles, which, if taken seriously, reduces all human effort to complete futility. According to Spengler, there are a series of civilizations, each repeating in considerable detail the pattern of its predecessors, each rising slowly to maturity and then sinking into inevitable decay; the decay of our civilization began in 1914, and nothing that we can do will arrest the march of our world towards senility. This theory, fortunately, is as groundless as it is gloomy. The previous cycles require a very artificial arrangement of history, with too much emphasis on some facts and too little on others. Even if this were not the case, the instances of past civilizations are too few to warrant an induction. And it ignores the qualitative novelties introduced by science, as well as the quantitative novelty resulting from the world-wide character of modern wars, involving the possibility of a world-wide domination of the victors. The Preacher said there is no new thing under the sun, but he would not have said so if he could have seen a large power station or a battle in the stratosphere. These things, it must be confessed, might not have prevented him from saying "all is vanity," but that is a different question.

There are things to be learnt from history, but they are not simple general formulae, which can only be made plausible by missing out half the facts. The men who make up philosophies of history may be dismissed as inventors of mythologies. There remain two very different functions that history can perform. On the one hand it may seek for comparatively small and humble generalizations such as might form a beginning of a science (as opposed to a philosophy) of history. On the other hand, it can, by the study of individuals, seek to combine the merits of drama or epic poetry with the merit of truth. I am not prepared to put either of these two functions above the other. They are very different, they appeal to different types of mind, and they demand different methods. One might take "Middletown" and Plutarch's Lives as illustrative of the two types of history. I should not wish to be deprived of either, but the satisfactions that they offer are as far asunder as the poles. The one views man objectively, as the heavenly bodies are viewed by an astronomer; the other appeals to imagination, and aims at giving us the kind of knowledge of men that a practiced horseman has of horses—a knowledge felt rather than expressed, which it would be impossible to translate into the language of science, but which is none the less useful in practical affairs.

Scientific history is a modern invention. Let us therefore leave it aside for the present, and consider what is to be gained by reading some of the great historians of the past.

Herodotus, who is called the Father of History, is worth reading for a number of reasons. In the first place, he is full of amusing stories. Almost at the beginning of the book, there is the story of the vain king Candaules, who regretted that no one but himself knew fully the beauty of his Queen, for which he wished to be envied. So he hid his Prime Minister Gyges behind a curtain, where he would see the Queen going naked to the bath. But she saw his feet sticking out, and complained that he had offered her a mortal indignity. Then and there she made him a speech: "Only two courses are open to you to expiate your offense," she said, "either you must die the death, or you must kill the King and marry me." Gyges had no difficulty in making his choice, and became the founder of the dynasty that ended with Croesus. Herodotus is full of such stories, from which he is not deterred by any scruples as to the dignity of history. Nor does respect for fact cause him to abstain from drama; the account of the defeat of Croesus by Cyrus is a fascinating tale, though obviously in part legend rather than history.

To any one who enjoys anthropology, Herodotus is interesting from his description of various barbarian customs as they existed in his day. Sometimes he is merely repeating travellers' tales, but very often he is confirmed by modern research. His survey of the nations and races known to him is leisurely and ample, and affords an admirable introduction to the ancient world for a previously ignorant reader.

The main theme of his history is the conflict of Europe and Asia, culminating, for his time, in the defeats of the Persians at Marathon and Salamis. Throughout all the subsequent centuries this swaying battle has continued. Salamis marked the end of the westward expansion of the Asiatics in Greek times; then came European conquest of Asia by the Macedonians and Romans, culminating in the time of Trajan, and followed by a long period of Asiatic ascendency. Limits were set to the extent of Asiatic conquest by the defeat of Attila at Chalons in the 5th Century and of the Moors at Tours in the 8th; the last great Asiatic victory was the conquest of Constantinople in 1453. In subsequent centuries, Europe had unquestioned superiority through scientific technique; the first sign of a contrary movement was the defeat of Russia by the Japanese in the war of 1904-5. How far this contrary movement will go it is impossible to guess, for, though Japan will no doubt be defeated, China and India will succeed to it as champions of Asia. All these vast secular movements come within the framework suggested by Herodotus.

Thucydides, the second of the great historians, has a smaller theme than that of Herodotus, but treats it with more art and also with a more careful regard for accuracy. His subject is the conflict of Athens and Sparta in the Peloponnesian war. His history, as Cornford has pointed out, is modeled on Greek tragedy: Athens, his own beloved city, which was finally defeated, is like the typical hero, driven by Fate and overweening pride to a disastrous but not inglorious end. His writing is severe, and confined strictly to what is relevant; there are no gossipy digressions, and there is little that is amusing. But there is a presentation, full of epic grandeur, of the spectacle of men driven by Destiny into folly, choosing wrongly over and over again when a right choice would have brought victory, becoming wicked through exasperation, and falling at last into irretrievable ruin. The theme is one that appealed to the Greek mind. A great impersonal Power, called indifferently Fate or Justice or Necessity, ruled the world, and was superior to the gods. Whatever person or country or thing overstepped the ordained boundaries suffered the punishment of pride. This was the real religion of the Greeks, and Thucydides in his history magnificently illustrated it.

Plutarch, ever since the renaissance, has been the most influential of ancient historians, not indeed among the writers on history, for he is by no means reliable, but among practical statesmen and political theorists. To take only two examples: Rousseau and

Alexander Hamilton owed the bent of their minds largely to him; his maxims supplied Rousseau with doctrines, and his heroes supplied Hamilton with ambitions. A reader to whom he has hitherto been merely a great name is likely to be surprised to find that he is an easy-going gossipy writer, who cannot resist a good story, and except in a few instances is quite willing to relate and even exaggerate the weaknesses of his heroes. He tells for instance how Mark Antony, when he was already an important official, gave offense by travelling everywhere with a third-rate actress, whom he inflicted even upon the most rigidly respectable provincials. (This was before he had reached the point at which he could aspire to Queens.) He tells how Caesar, as a young man, got into trouble for reading a love-letter from Brutus's mother during a meeting of the Senate, where no one was allowed to read anything. And then he goes on to portray Caesar in the aspect of slightly ridiculous pomposity that Shakespeare has preserved. His heroes are not statuesque figures of perfection; they are concrete men, who could have existed even if they never in fact did.

There are many admirable ways of writing history; three of them are illustrated by Herodotus, Thucydides, and Plutarch; a fourth is illustrated by Gibbon. Gibbon, it must be admitted, has grave defects. His erudition, by modern standards, is inadequate; his characters, even when they are barbarians, have an 18th Century flavor, like Voltaire's cannibals; princes, wars, and politics crowd out common men and economic facts more than the modern reader could wish. But when all this is allowed he remains both a great and a delightful writer.

His wit and irony—particularly when he uses them

to contemn superstition—are inimitable. But his chief virtue is that, although his portraits of individuals are often disappointing, his sense of the march of great events is sure and unerring. No one has ever presented the pageant of history better than he has done. To treat in one book the whole period from the 2nd Century to the 15th was a colossal undertaking, but he never lost sight of the unity of his theme, or of the proportions to be preserved among its several parts. This required a grasp of a great whole which is beyond the power of most men, and which, for all his shortcomings, puts Gibbon in the first rank among historians.

But it is not enough to read the great historians; much that is important, much that is delightful and amusing, is only to be discovered by discursive reading of biographies and memoirs. The professors must not prevent us from realizing that history is full of fun, and that the most bizarre things really happen. I have found that the greatest pleasures to be derived from history come only after one knows some period rather well, for then each new fact fits into its place in the jig-saw puzzle. Until one knows much intimate detail about a prominent man, it is impossible to judge whether he was really as great as he appears or not. Some great men become greater the more they are studied; I should mention Spinoza and Lincoln as instances. Napoleon, on the other hand, becomes, at close quarters, a ridiculous figure. Perhaps it was not his fault that on the night of his wedding to Josephine her pug-dog bit him in the calf as he was getting into bed, but on many occasions on which he appeared in an unfavorable light the whole blame was clearly his. In the course of one of his many quarrels with Talleyrand, he twitted his foreign secretary with being a cripple and having an unfaithful wife; after he was gone, Talleyrand shrugged his shoulders, turned to the bystanders, and remarked: "What a pity that such a great man should have such bad manners." His marriage to Marie Louise was celebrated by proxy, and he travelled to the frontiers of France to meet her. A magnificent ceremonial was arranged, including a state banquet at which all the great men and grand ladies in Napoleon's orbit were to be present. The dinner-hour came; it passed, and still the Emperor and Empress did not appear. The Court Chamberlain was in perplexity and despair. At last, by discreet inquiries, he discovered that Napoleon could not wait till after dinner to enjoy the favors of an Emperor's daughter. The Czar Alexander took his measure, and deceived him completely by pretending to be a simple-minded youth. At the height of his apparent friendship with Napoleon, he wrote to his mother to say, "he laughs best who laughs last." In the correspondence of the two Emperors, all the skill is on the side of Alexander, all the bombast on the side of Napoleon. It is a pity that historians have failed to emphasize the ridiculous sides of Napoleon, for he became a myth and a legend, inspiring admiration of military conquest and the cult of the military superman. His effect was particularly bad on the Germans, who at the same time admired him and wished for revenge on account of the humiliations which he had inflicted on them. If they could have laughed at him, they could have had their revenge at less cost to mankind.

The meetings of eminent men of very different types are often amusing and sometimes surprising. No two men could have been further apart than Robert Owen and the Czar Nicholas. Robert Owen was the founder of Socialism, a passionate Atheist, and during part of his life a subversive agitator. Nicholas was a ferocious tyrant, whose reign was one of black reaction; it was he who sent Dostoyevsky to Siberia and Bakunin to the prison of Peter and Paul. One would not have expected these two men to like one another, and yet their one and only meeting was most cordial; it is true it took place before Nicholas had become an Emperor and Owen a Socialist. Nicholas travelled all the way to New Lanark in Scotland to visit Owen's model factory, saw everything, approved everything, and invited the philanthropist to found similar factories in Russia. Owen was so charmed that he gave all his plate to his distinguished visitor—to the no small indignation of Mrs. Owen. What they thought of each other in later life history does not record.

On the other hand, Goethe and Beethoven, who might have been expected to like each other, did not, because, when the composer visited the poet at Weimar, the poet tried to give instruction as to court etiquette, and Beethoven indignantly insisted on behaving as he chose.

A great deal of nonsense has been written about Aristotle and Alexander, because, as both were great men, and Aristotle was Alexander's tutor, it is supposed that the tutor must have greatly influenced the pupil. Hegel goes so far as to say that Alexander's career shows the value of philosophy, since his practical wisdom may be attributed to his teacher. In fact there is not the faintest evidence that Aristotle had any effect at all on Alexander, who hated his father, and was rebellious against every one whom his father set in authority over him. There are certain letters professing to be from Alexander to Aristotle, but they are generally considered spurious. In fact, the two men ignored each other. While Alexander was conquering the East, and causing the era of City States to be succeeded by that of great empires, Aristotle continued to write treatises on politics which never mentioned what was taking place, but discussed minutely the constitutions of various cities which were no longer important. It is a mistake to suppose that great men who are contemporaries are likely to be quick to recognize each other's greatness; the opposite happens much more frequently. Voltaire and Frederick the Great, after a brief friendship, became bitter enemies. Frederick wrote French verses which Voltaire praised insufficiently; Voltaire made fun of Maupertuis, whom Frederick had made perpetual President of the Berlin Academy; and finally Voltaire fled to France carrying with him a manuscript volume of Frederick's lampoons on Madame de Pompadour. After these events, Voltaire's penchant for monarchs vented itself in adulation of Catherine the Great.

History is invaluable in increasing our knowledge of human nature, because it shows how people may be expected to behave in new situations. Many prominent men and women are completely ordinary in character, and only exceptional in their circumstances. The behavior of the ordinary married woman is closely circumscribed by prudential considerations. She wishes to be more respected than her neighbors; she must not bring disgrace on her husband for fear of loss of income; she cannot ill-treat her children in any overt way, for fear of getting a bad name. There have, however, been a few women who could do as they chose; they were Empresses regnant. If they are to be taken as showing what women would do if they dared, we

ought to be thankful for social restraints. Most of them
have murdered or imprisoned their sons, and often
their husbands; almost all have had innumerable lovers. Catherine the Great—"The Semiramis of the
North," as Voltaire called her—when she grew too
old and fat had to pay her lovers enormous salaries.
Even then they would attempt to fly across the fron-
tier, but if they were caught it was the worse for them.
It is interesting to speculate as to which of our respectable neighbors would behave in this way if they were
Empresses.

As soon as you know the general outline of history
of some period, it becomes agreeable and profitable to
read the letters and memoirs of the time. Not only do
they contain much intimate detail which makes it possible to realize that the men concerned really lived,
but there is the advantage that the writers did not
know what was going to happen, as the historians do.
Historians are apt to represent what occurred as inevitable, so that it comes to seem as if contemporaries
must have foreseen coming events. Everything becomes much more vivid when one sees the mistakes
and perplexities of those who could only guess at the
outcome, and often guessed wrong. One is surprised,
often, by preoccupation with small matters when great
things are happening. When Napoleon's return from
Elba compelled the Bourbons to fly, Louis Phillippe
wrote innumerable letters of lamentation, not about
public affairs, but about his children's whooping cough.
When Lord Granville Levison Gower had to fly from
Austerlitz, what worried him most was that the roads
were rough and his coach had defective springs. When
Cicero sailed from Italy to escape the proscription of

the second triumvirate, he turned back because he decided that sea-sickness was worse than death.

But it is time to be done with frivolities and consider some of the graver aspects of history. There are so many that it is difficult to know with which to begin; perhaps at this time it is natural to think first of military history. I do not mean accounts of the details of battles, of which there is far too much in most books of history; I mean the effects of changing modes of warfare on the general life of the community, and the relation between military and other forms of success. War is usually romanticized, but is in fact a business like another. Most people imagine that Joan of Arc had a great deal to do with the recovery of France after the defeats inflicted by the English under Henry V. I had thought so myself until I discovered that the real cause of French success was the growing importance of artillery. The English had depended upon their archers, who were capable of defeating the French knights; but against cannon they were powerless. Throughout western Europe, during the 60 years or so following Joan of Arc, the new form of warfare enabled kings to subdue the turbulent barons who had caused centuries of anarchy. Despotic government and civil order were both brought into western Europe by gunpowder. Will both be brought to the world as a whole by the aeroplane? Or will it bring only one of the two, and if so which?

The French Revolution introduced a new kind of war, one in which the whole nation participates enthusiastically because it believes that it has something of value to defend. Wars had been an affair of kings or of small aristocracies; the armies were composed of

mercenaries, and the general population looked on
with indifference. If Louis XIV conquered some part
of Germany, that was unpleasant for a few Princes
and their hangers-on, but it made very little difference
to most people. But when all the reactionaries of
Europe set to work in concert to destroy revolutionary
France and restore the Bourbons, every peasant who
had been freed from feudal burdens and had acquired
some portion of his seigneur's land felt that he had
something to fight for. And all the scientific intellect
of France set to work to devise new methods of making more effective explosives, or otherwise helping the
war effort. The result astonished the world, and
French successes were welcomed by large sections of
Germany and Italy. After Napoleon's tyranny had
turned the former friends of France into enemies, Germany, in the war of 1813, fought a similar popular
war, and this time with more lasting success. From that
time until the present day, governments have increasingly realized the necessity of making wars popular,
and have used the potent weapon of popular education to that end. Democracy, as a form of government,
has the advantage of making everybody a participant
in war. I think it may be doubted (and I see that
Goebbels agrees with me in this) whether a country
under an undemocratic regime would be as unmoved
in disaster as England was in 1940. This is one of the
strongest reasons for expecting democracy to survive.

It is sometimes said that victory in war is always due
to superior economic resources, but history shows that
this is by no means invariably the case. The Romans,
at the beginning of the Punic Wars, had much smaller
resources than the Carthaginians, and yet they were
victorious. When the Roman Empire fell, it was over-

run by German and Arab invaders who had nothing on their side except valor and greed. The decadence of Spain in the late 16th and the 17th Centuries must be attributed almost entirely to stupidity and fanaticism, not to lack of resources. In the present war, in spite of superior resources, the United Nations have lost France, the Malay Peninsula, Burma, the Philippines, the Dutch East Indies, Rumanian oil and Ukrainian wheat; no doubt they will recover them, but their loss shows what can be done by nations which devote all their energies to war. All that can be said is that, given equal skill and equal resolution, the side which has superior economic resources will win in the long run.

Quite recent times have, however, introduced an important change in warfare, analogous to that brought about by gunpowder. Just as gunpowder gave the king supremacy over the barons, so modern weapons have given supremacy to the great industrial nations as compared to those that are small or unindustrialized. In the old days, a small nation might hold out against a large one for years; now it can hold out for at most a few weeks. The great industrial nations, in order of their industrial power, are the United States, Germany, Russia, Great Britain, and Japan; the rest are nowhere (except that China has shown astonishing strength in defense). All first-class power in war is concentrated among these five; if two of them are defeated, it will be concentrated among three. I think any student of the history of warfare must conclude that the ultimate issue will be the holding of all military power by one government, which will probably be a federation of several national governments. There will be prejudices and psychological obstacles to be overcome, but the mere pressure of military fact must become irresistible in the end—though after how long a time and how many wars I do not venture to predict.

A particularly important department of history is economic history. Unfortunately, it was hardly at all studied in ancient or medieval times, so that the facts are often hard to ascertain. It has, however, as compared to older kinds of history, the merit of concentrating on the common man as opposed to the exceptional individual. Did the Egyptian peasant at the time when the pyramids were being built get enough to eat? How intolerable was the lot of slaves in Roman times? Who was exploited to supply the income that enabled Plato to be bland? What went wrong with the economic structure of the Roman Empire at the end of the 2nd Century A. D.? How well off was the average inhabitant of a prosperous commercial city in the middle ages? Was the lot of the agricultural laborer under a pre-industrial aristrocratic regime better or worse than that of a factory worker in the early stages of industrialism? Such questions are interesting, and economic history supplies at least hints as to the answers.

The economic historians, it must be said, are somewhat addicted to stereotypes. Almost any book of economic history, no matter what the region and the period dealt with, will contain some pages of lamentation to the following effect: "At this period the ancient yeomanry was sinking into decay; the land was mortgaged to rapacious urban money-lenders, to whom the cultivators of the soil became actually or virtually enslaved. The old aristocracy, which, for all its faults, had had some sense of public responsibility, was being replaced by a new plutocracy, ignorant of agricultural needs, and anxious only to extract the maximum of revenue in the shortest possible time. Ruined and dispossessed yeomen flocked into the cities, where they became an element of proletarian unrest, and apt material for the machinations of demagogues. The old simple pieties decayed, to be replaced by skepticism and violence." You will find this, or something like it, in accounts of Greece at any time from that of Hesiod onwards; again in descriptions of Italy after the Punic Wars; again in accounts of England under the Tudors. In our day writers are more diffuse; the corresponding account of California fills two long books, "Grapes of Wrath" and Norris's "Octopus." What the historians say is no doubt true in the main as regards the evils of their own period, but it is often mistaken in supposing other periods to have been better.

This point of view is in part a product of specialization. A man who knows much about a certain period, and little about the immediately preceding period, imagines—partly because of a well established literary convention—that the evils he observes in the period with which he is familiar were new. In fact, agriculturists have at all times been liable to fall into debt, as a result of optimism and bad harvests. The men who can lend money during a famine are likely to be urban, since otherwise they also would be poor. Aristocracies at all times have been addicted to certain vices, such as gambling, fighting, and over-building, which have compelled them to part with their land to new men. The old simple pieties were never so simple or so pious as historians pretend. Throughout the middle ages, barons and eminent ecclesiastics borrowed from Jews, and when they could no longer pay the interest they instituted a pogrom. At the beginning of the modern age, capital became largely Christian, and therefore pogroms of capitalists were no longer tolerated. To describe this change as a decay of the "old simple pieties" is somewhat misleading. It had, however, the important effect of causing abandonment of the condemnation of "usury" (i. e. interest), a condemnation which, though supported by the authority of Aristotle, ceased to be effective as soon as creditors were no longer mainly Jews. But Nazi Germany shows that it is still possible to revive the medieval pattern; the party programme, like the churchmen of the middle ages, condemns alike Jews and interest.

Economic history, in one of its aspects, represents a perennial conflict between city and country. Culture has at all times been mainly urban, and piety mainly rural. In antiquity, almost everything of importance to posterity was urban. Greek philosophy and science began in the rich commercial cities of Asia Minor and Sicily; thence they passed to Athens, and thence, finally, to Alexandria. The Romans who fought in the Punic wars were largely agriculturists, and had very little culture; but after victory had made the Romans rich, they left agriculture to slaves and subject nations, while they themselves took to Greek culture and Oriental luxury. Commerce between the different parts of the Roman Empire rapidly increased, and reached a maximum in the 2nd Century A. D. Great cities flourished, even in regions which are now desert; their ruins astonish the traveller in the parched wastes of North Africa. Throughout the long period from 600 B. C. to 200 A. D., the City was dominant over the country, which was not the case before and after those dates. The changes are reflected in religious conceptions: Paradise, in Genesis, is rural, and so is Dante's Earthly

Paradise; in the intervening period, men's aspirations are embodied in Plato's Republic, the New Jerusalem, and the City of God, all of which are urban.

The barbarian invasions destroyed the Roman roads and made travel unsafe; they therefore put an almost complete end to commerce, and compelled each small area to raise its own food. At the same time they established a rural aristocracy of conquerors, who gradually developed the feudal system. The lay culture of the middle ages, except in Italy, was rural and aristocratic, not urban and commercial. This rural character survived in England, Germany, and Russia until quite recent times. The tone of English poetry was set by Shakespeare's "native wood-notes wild"; Bismarck was militantly bucolic; and Tolstoy held that all virtue is connected with the land. But the industrial revolution made this point of view a mere survival; though John Bull is a farmer, the typical Englishman of the present day is urban.

In America the conflict of town and country begins with the opposition between Hamilton and Jefferson; it continues with Andrew Jackson, who secured a temporary victory for the rural population; passing through the Populists and W. J. Bryan, it persists in our day in the struggle between the Farm Bloc and the anti-inflationists. In Russia, since the revolution, the conflict has taken fiercer forms. The New Economic Policy, in Lenin's last years, was a concession to the peasants, but Stalin, by ruthless methods, finally secured the victory for the urban party. These conflicts are illuminated by being seen in their historical perspective.

Modern views as to the relation of economic facts to general culture have been profoundly affected by the theory, first explicitly stated by Marx, that the mode of production of an age (and to a lesser degree the mode of exchange) is the ultimate cause of the character of its politics, laws, literature, philosophy, and religion. Like all sweeping theories, this doctrine is misleading if accepted as a dogma, but it is valuable if used as a means of suggesting hypotheses. It has indubitably a large measure of truth, though not so much as Marx believed. R. H. Tawney's "Religion and the Rise of Capitalism," a most valuable and interesting book, illustrates with a wealth of illuminating detail a theory which is in some sense the converse of Marx's doctrine. Tawney is concerned to trace a connection between Protestantism and capitalism, in which, largely by way of individualism, Protestantism is the cause and capitalism the effect: *laissez-faire* in theology may be regarded as the source of *laissez-faire* in business. It is undeniable that modern capitalism began in Protestant countries, but I doubt whether the connection is quite what Tawney represents it as being.

In the 17th Century, England and Holland were the leading commercial countries. Both were Protestant, and both had abundant political reasons for their Protestantism. The Pope had bestowed the East Indies and Brazil on Portugal, and the rest of the Western hemisphere on Spain. This did not suit Northern nations that wished to trade with India and establish colonies in America. Moreover Spain was a danger to both; Holland owed its existence to a successful revolt against Spain, and England owed its survival to the defeat of the Spanish Armada. Protestantism went naturally with hostility to Spain, which was the leading Catholic Power. There were therefore ample secular reasons for the Protestantism of England and Holland. Their commercial success, however, was due to their excellence as seamen and to their geographical position. Perhaps success colored their religion, which was in some ways different in temper from German Lutheranism. But I doubt whether Protestantism was actually in any important degree a *cause* of the capitalist doctrines which were naturally engendered by commerce and manufactures. In an earlier age, North Italy had led the world in economic development, but had not quarrelled with the Pope, and had not acquired what Tawney regards as the Protestant mentality. I do not deny an element of truth in his thesis, but I think it is less than he supposes.

To return to Marx: The most important error in his theory, to my mind, is that it ignores intelligence as a cause. Men and apes, in the same environment, have different methods of securing food: men practice agriculture, not because of some extra-human dialectic compelling them to do so, but because intelligence shows them its advantages. The industrial revolution might have taken place in antiquity if Greek intelligence had remained what it was at its best. To this it is customary to reply that slave labor, being cheap, removed the incentive to the invention of labor-saving devices. The facts do not bear out this view. Modern methods of production began in the cotton industry, not only in spinning and weaving, which employed "free" labor, but also in the gathering of cotton, which was the work of slaves. Moreover no slaves were ever cheaper than the wretched children whom the Lancashire manufacturers employed in the factories of the early 19th Century, where they had to work 14 or 16 hours a day, for little more than board and lodging, till they died. (It must be remembered that the death of a slave was an economic loss to his owner, but the death of a wage-earner is not.) Yet it was these same ruthless employers who were the pioneers of the industrial revolution, because their heads were better than their hearts. Without intelligence, men would never have learnt to economize hand labor by the help of machines.

I do not wish to suggest that intelligence is something that arises spontaneously, in some mystical uncaused manner. Obviously it has its causes, and obviously these causes are in part to be sought in the social environment. But in part the causes are biological and individual. These are as yet little understood, though Mendelianism has made a beginning. Men of supreme ability are just as definitely congenitally different from the average as are the feeble-minded. And without supreme ability fundamental advances in methods of production cannot take place.

There is a modern school of sociology, which professes to be more strictly scientific than any other, and which is, at least to some extent, an outcome of Marx's doctrines. According to this school, sociology can only become truly scientific by observing men in the mass rather than as individuals, and by observing only their bodily behavior without any attempt at psychological interpretation. Up to a point, there is much to be said for this school. Undoubtedly pleasure in what is dramatic has caused both the readers and the writers of history to lay too much stress on individuals; undoubtedly, also, there is an element of risk in any psychological interpretation of physical behavior. As the poet says:

> It was all very well to dissemble your love,
> But why did you kick me downstairs?

The school in question will note only the kicking, and will not inquire whether it was caused by dissembled love or by hatred. At any rate we can agree so far, that it is a good thing to record the indubitable facts of overt behavior before embarking upon the doubtful sea of inward motivation.

A book such as "Middletown," although its authors do not subscribe to the theory we are examining, is one which the advocates of the theory can approve, and which shows that much valuable work may be suggested by the theory. Some 50 years ago, Charles Booth's "Life and Labour of the People in London" performed, on a much larger scale, the same sort of task for London; it was an immensely valuable book, which inspired reforms that greatly increased the well-being of the poorer sections of the population in London. To the reformer, if he is to act wisely, such surveys of the average lives of men, women, and children are immeasurably useful.

They are, however, a means, not an end in themselves; when regarded as an end, they are in danger of losing their usefulness. To begin with, the objection to psychological interpretations is foolish. Why do we object to poverty and illness? Because they cause suffering, which is a mental phenomenon. To a purely external observation, poverty and illness should be just as satisfactory as prosperity and good health. When the astronomer observes the stars, he does not have to consider whether their condition is "good" or "bad," because we do not believe that they can feel; but human beings are different, and a sociology which ignores their feelings is leaving out what is most essential. We do not wish to reform the solar system, but we do wish to reform the social system if we have any sympathy with suffering. And only psychological considerations can show us what reforms are desirable.

From a purely scientific point of view, the theory seems to me mistaken in minimizing the effect of individuals. It often happens that large opposing social forces are in approximate momentary equilibrium, and that a comparatively small force may decide which shall be victorious, just as a very small force on a watershed may decide whether water shall flow into the Atlantic or the Pacific. The Russian Revolution would have been very different without Lenin, and it was a very small force that decided the Germans to permit his return to Russia. The Duke of Wellington remarked about the battle of Waterloo: "It was a damned nice thing. I do believe if I had not been there we should not have won." Probably he was right. Such instances show that the main course of great events may sometimes depend upon the actions of an individual.

This, of course, is regrettable from the point of view of those who are impatient to turn history into a science. But in fact, while some aspects of history can be made more or less scientific, and while it is important to do this wherever it is possible, the material is too complex to be reduced to scientific laws at present, and probably for centuries to come. There is too much that, to our ignorance, appears as chance, and too great a likelihood of the intrusion of incalculable forces. There is nothing genuinely scientific in a premature attempt to *seem* scientific.

This brings me to another department of history, namely, the history of culture, conceived in its widest sense, to include religion, art, philosophy, and science. This is a fascinating subject, when it is treated without the solemnity and humbug in which it has been steeped by pedantic professors. The official view—which every student must adopt if he is to obtain good grades—is that certain famous men were great and good, and must on no account be criticized, while certain others were clever but wrong-headed, and committed foolish mistakes which are obvious to every tyro. Yet others, who to an unprejudiced eye appear far from contemptible, are to be not even mentioned, because their ideas were shocking. Even those who are singled out for the highest praise must be so misinterpreted as to become dull and acceptable to the commonplace men whose business it is to praise them. Above all, no idea must be admitted which could cause even a moment's discomfort to complacent middle age.

Not so are great men to be conceived, and not such is the monument to be raised to them in our thoughts. The pedant, convinced that he himself possesses all wisdom, and comfortable in the security of his job, praises the men whom he pretends to study by pretending that they agree with him, and specially commends whatever occasional sententious humbug they may have permitted themselves. He is convinced that the truly great are always "serene," that they see how, in mysterious ways, good comes out of evil, and that, speaking generally, they help us to bear with fortitude the misfortunes of others. The generous young, exposed in almost every university of the world to this desiccated abomination, are apt to reject with scorn all the conventionally great names. Take, for example, Shakespeare, whose supposed "serenity" is the theme of endless academic nonsense. Here are a few examples of his "serenity":

When we are born we cry, that we are come
To this great stage of fools.

Again:

As flies to us are we to the gods,
They kill us for their sport.

Again:

You taught me language, and my profit on't
Is, I know to curse.

And well known as it is, I cannot omit the great speech in *Macbeth:*

Tomorrow and tomorrow and tomorrow
Creeps in this petty pace from day to day
To the last syllable of recorded time,
And all our yesterdays have lighted fools
The way to dusty death. Out, out, brief candle.
Life's but a walking shadow, a poor player,
Who struts and frets his hour upon the stage,
And then is heard no more. It is a tale
Told by an idiot, full of sound and fury,
Signifying nothing.

No, the greatest men have not been "serene." They have had, it is true, an ultimate courage, a power of creating beauty where nature has put only horror, which may, to a petty mind, appear like serenity. But their courage has had to surpass that of common men, because they have seen deeper into the indifference of nature and the cruelty of man. To cover up these things with comfortable lies is the business of cowards; the business of great men is to see them with inflexible clarity, and yet to think and feel nobly. And in the degree in which we can all be great, this is the business of each one of us.

But all this, the reader may feel, is a digression from the history of culture. I cannot agree. In the history of culture, the material is vast, and selection is necessary. Selection must be guided, at least in part, by a sense of values: we must have some touchstone by which to decide who deserves to be remembered. This cannot, it is true, be our sole principle of selection; some men must be studied because of their influence. Even if we have no very high opinion of Mahomet (say), we cannot ignore him, because a large section of mankind believes in him. But even then standards are necessary if the history of culture is to be studied with any profit; we must not indiscriminately admire whoever has been influential, for if we do we may find ourselves worshiping Satan. The ultimate value of culture is to suggest standards of good and evil which science alone cannot supply, and this should be remembered in all our study of culture in the past and in the present.

To me, as one whose life has been mainly devoted to philosophical speculation, the most interesting part of the history of culture is the history of philosophy, particularly in its relation to religion. Philosophy began among the Greeks as a revolt against religion, embodying the skepticism of men who, in the course of commerce, had been brought into contact with many beliefs and customs, and had therefore come to demand something more than tribal tradition as a basis for their own creed. Their rationalism was, of course, imperfect; even the most free-thinking among them retained the belief in Fate or cosmic justice of which I spoke earlier. But their rationality, where it existed, was more surprising than their irrationality where it survived. They rejected the Olympian gods, they formed the conception of universal causation, and they tried to discover ways in which the existing universe could have evolved in accordance with natural laws. For the first time in human history, Reason was proclaimed to be paramount, and everything was submitted to its scrutiny, in principle if not in fact. Surviving prejudices survived because they were unnoticed; if any one had pointed out that they were prejudices, the early Ionian philosophers would have abandoned them.

But Greek philosophy did not continue to live up to this brilliant beginning; there was a serpent in the philosophic paradise, and his name was Pythagoras. The Orphic religion, which had revivalist features, had captivated many previously rationalistic Greeks, and a form of Orphism was introduced by Pythagoras into philosophy, which ceased to be an honest attempt to understand the world, and became a search for salvation through intoxication. Orphism was an offshoot of the worship of Bacchus, but sought to substitute a spiritual intoxication for the frankly alcoholic intoxication of the original cult. From that day to this, there has been thought to be something divine about muddleheadedness, provided it had the quality of spiritual intoxication; a wholly sober view of the world has been thought to show a limited and pedestrian mind. From Pythagoras this outlook descended to Plato, from Plato to Christian theologians, from them, in a new form, to Rousseau and the romantics and the myriad purveyors of nonsense who flourish wherever men and women are tired of the truth.

There is, however, in our day, a powerful antidote

to nonsense, which hardly existed in earlier times—I mean science. Science cannot be ignored or rejected, because it is bound up with modern technique; it is essential alike to prosperity in peace and to victory in war. This is, perhaps, from an intellectual point of view, the most hopeful feature of our age, and the one which makes it most likely that we shall escape complete submersion in some new or old superstition.

One of the most fascinating studies in the history of culture is the gradual building up of the Catholic synthesis, which was completed in the 13th Century. In the Church as it existed at the time of the fall of the Western Empire (i. e. in the 5th Century) there were elements derived from three sources, Jewish, Greek and Roman. The Church took over from the Jews their sacred books and sacred history, their belief in a Messiah (whom the Christians, but not the Jews, believed to have already appeared), their somewhat fierce morality, and their intolerance of all religions but one. The Hellenic element appeared especially in the realm of dogma. St. John, St. Paul, and the Fathers gradually developed, by adaptations of Greek philosophy, an elaborate theology, wholly foreign to the Jewish spirit. St. John's gospel, unlike Matthew, Mark, and Luke, shows the early stages of Christian Hellenistic philosophy. The Fathers, especially Origen and St. Augustine, made Platonism an integral part of Christian thought; it is astonishing how much of essential Christian doctrine St. Augustine confesses to having found in Plato. As soon as the Empire became Christian, the bishops acquired administrative and judicial functions; the oecumenial councils promoted by the Emperors supplied the beginnings of a central authority, though at first only in matters of doctrine. Without the strength derived from Roman governmental methods, it is doubtful whether the Church could have survived the shock of the barbarian invasion.

In the centuries that followed, the Church, though imperfectly, represented Mediterranean culture, while the lay aristocracy represented Northern barbarism. The Church, at times, nearly lost its distinctive character, and almost became part and parcel of the feudal system. But this was prevented by the gradually increasing power of the Pope, and by papal insistence on clerical celibacy, which prevented Church lands from descending from father to son. From the beginning of the 11th to the end of the 13th Century, the Church gained rapidly in power, discipline, and learning; in the latter respect, Catholics still bow to the authority of St. Thomas Aquinas, whose word, on all philosophical questions, is law in all Catholic educational institutions. Yet Aquinas, in his day, was a bold innovator. Arabic influences caused him to prefer Aristotle to Plato, and on this account he was condemned by the universities of Paris and Oxford. This opposition to Aquinas and Aristotle (who was also condemned) has been forgotten, and Aristotle is now regarded by Catholics almost as if he were one of the Fathers. It is perhaps permissible, though in dubious taste, to question the efficacy of his cure for insomnia in elephants, but his mistakes in the doctrine of the syllogism must not be acknowledged. For this reason, modern logic is forbidden territory to Catholics.

The misfortunes of the Church in the 14th, 15th, and 16th centuries were so great that its survival might almost be claimed as a miracle. First came the Great Schism, during which there were two men who claimed to be Pope. No one knew which was the true Pope; each claimant excommunicated the other. One of these excommunications was valid, but which? Whichever was the true Pope must of course be right in proclaiming his rival to be a wicked man, but no one knew which was the Holy Father and which was an impudent impostor. This was awkward, and a potent cause of scandal. When at last the Schism was healed, the renaissance began, and the Popes lost sight of the interests of the Church to play the game of Italian power politics and fight to enlarge their secular dominions. A series of free-thinking, worldly, and licentious Popes, who taxed the faithful throughout the Catholic world to keep up their own pomp, so shocked Northern piety as in the end to produce the Reformation.

At first the Reformation carried everything before it in most countries north of the Alps. But the Catholic cause was rescued by Loyola, Charles V, and the Fuggers. Loyola founded the Jesuit Order, which secured power by zeal, cunning, and education. Charles V happened to combine under his sway the Empire, Spain, and the Netherlands. The rich banking house of the Fuggers had already lent him so much money that his success became vital to them; they therefore backed him with all their resources, and made him financially superior to his opponents. In the end they went bankrupt through lending to Hapsburgs, but by that time the Church was saved.

Does the past history of the Church give any basis for prophecy as to its future? Its misfortunes did not end in the 16th Century. The wars of the 18th Century, and the subsequent expansion of the United States, gave dominion to Protestants throughout all of the American Continent north of the Mexican border. France was vehemently anti-clerical during the Revolution, and again at the time of the rehabilitation of Dreyfus. The Russian Revolution was anti-Christian, and the Nazis have done all in their power to destroy the influence of the Church in Germany. Nevertheless, Catholics have considerable grounds for confidence in the future. Napoleon found it expedient to make peace with the Pope, and Napoleon III, until his downfall, preserved the temporal power by a French garrison in Rome. What France will be like after the war, it is impossible to know; but at present the leaders of all parties are pious Catholics. The Russian Government has abandoned its hostility to religion, and will no doubt, to please its allies, go further in its new direction. In Germany, when the Nazis fall, there will be danger of chaos, and the Catholic Church will be one of the few forces making for stability. In the United States, Catholics are already sufficiently powerful to control education in New York and Boston, and they were able to compel the State Department to be friendly to Franco during the Spanish Civil War. They make many converts, and breed much faster than Protestants. Statistics show that, unless some new factor enters in, they will have a majority in the United States in about 50 years. There is therefore every reason to expect that their power at the end of the present century will be greater than at any time since the French Revolution. For my part, I view this prospect with alarm.

Consideration of the Church naturally suggests a department of history which, in my opinion, has been too little studied; I mean, the history of organizations. An organization has a life of its own, and is apt to go through stages of youth, maturity, and old age, analogous to the stages in the life of an individual. I believe that by the study of organizations many useful though not infallible generalizations could be arrived at. There are organizations of many different kinds: Churches, political parties, educational institutions, business corporations, trade unions, and so on. In all ages of technical progress, there has been an increase of organization, and this is especially true of our own time. The number of things that an individual does by his own initiative alone is continually diminishing, and the number of things for which he depends on some organization is continually increasing. If you are an average citizen, you are born in a hospital and educated by the State; you earn your living by working for a corporation; your newspaper, your radio, your movie are supplied by rich companies; if you acquire a house, you probably borrow the purchase money, not from an individual, but from an organization; when you die, an insurance company relieves your widow's necessities. As a free and independent citizen of a democracy, and a member of the Sovereign People, you have a right, from time to time, to express a preference as between two men presented to you by two organizations called political parties, which jointly represent the interests of professional politicians. As an immortal soul, you can seek salvation in an organization called a Church, which probably holds property on condition of adhering to dogmas that have been fixed for centuries; if none of the existing Churches satisfies you, your neighbors view you with suspicion as an eccentric, their wives fight shy of your wife, and your business career suffers. From the cradle to the grave, and even (if the Churches are right) in the life to come, you are in the hands of organizations, which determine the degree to which you are permitted to pursue your own interests.

Now every one of these organizations has a twofold purpose, one public, and one private. The State, when it educates you, has the public object of supplying you with useful knowledge, and the private object of making you willing to pay taxes for the benefit of corrupt politicians. Your newspaper exists publicly to give the news, privately to give it in such a way as will further the interests of the proprietors. Your political party has a public program, which is represented as being advantageous to the nation; but if you are neither young nor naive you know that the party, if victorious, is likely to consider that the program has served its purpose, which was to secure public money for one group of men rather than another. As for the Churches —but hush! at this point we must draw the line; no Church dignitary, I am sure, ever considers for a moment anything but the eternal welfare of his flock.

The study of the history of organizations shows that, from ignorance of the laws of their development, the idealistic efforts of many of the best and greatest of mankind have been wasted in directions which proved only harmful. Take, for instance, the Franciscan Order. It would be difficult to find in all history a more lovable man than St. Francis; he loved with a spontaneous love not only all mankind, but beasts and birds, the sun and the stars and the wind; his virtue was so spontaneous that he was always happy. His faith, no doubt, was somewhat simpleminded: he made a long and dangerous journey to see the Sultan, whom he hoped to convert to Christianity. But at any rate this attempt was less harmful than the equally futile method of the Crusades. He founded the Franciscan Order in the hope of spreading his own spirit of brotherly love; believing that there should be no opportunities of self-seeking, he adopted the traditional vows of chastity, poverty, and obedience. His immediate successor wallowed in luxury and rebelled against the Pope; *his* successors became recruiting sergeants in the savage wars of Guelfs and Gibellines, and together with the Dominicans administered the atrocious persecutions of the Inquisition. For a time, a minority of Franciscans, of whom William of Ockham was nearly the last, remained true to the spirit of their founder; but after the 14th Century it would be difficult to point to any benefit that mankind has owed to the existence of the Order.

There is nothing surprising in this development; if the Saint had had more worldly wisdom he would have foreseen it. Under the aegis of an honored name abominations are possible which, otherwise, would cause disastrous opprobrium. In the minds of many pious Japanese, national misdeeds are excused by the name of Buddha. It is superfluous to speak of the countless pogroms, persecutions, and witch-hunts that have been considered sanctified by the name of Christ. One might come nearer home, and point out how the name of Lincoln became, in the corrupt era that followed the Civil War, a shield to protect a gang of shameless miscreants. All these are gloomy reflections, but I am not content to draw a moral of lazy cynicism. The correct moral is that the evolution of organizations should be studied, with a view to discovering how to avoid the evils that we have been considering.

Some organizations succeed throughout a long period in fulfilling their original object; others soon fail. The

Royal Society, founded in the 17th Century for the promotion of science, has continued ever since to contain all the best British men of science among its Fellows; on the other hand, the Royal Academy has failed notoriously to recognize the best painters. In France, similarly, the *Institut* has adequately recognized scientific merit, while the Academy has excluded most of the best literary men. The reason, of course, is that scientific merit is more indubitable than artistic and literary merit. Saintliness is even harder to recognize than artistic excellence, for hypocrites throughout the ages have perfected the technique of protective imitation. Consequently an organization which can only do good if its leaders are saints is sure to begin to do harm before long. This is an important truth, which saints are slow to realize.

There are three things to be considered about an organization: what it offers to the public, what it offers to its own rank and file, and what it offers to its leaders. The last of these too often, in practice, outweighs the other two. This applies in many different fields. A man, let us say, offers for sale the finest soap on the market. By skillful advertisement he causes the public to believe him; he then sells his invention to a company; the public discovers its mistake and the company goes bankrupt, but the inventor of the soap retains his fortune. When I was young, it was the custom in certain South American countries for dictators to plunder the public until they provoked a revolution; they invested the proceeds abroad, and had at all times a fast ship with steam up waiting for them in the harbor of their capital. At the moment when the revolution began they fled to Paris and lived happily ever after. These dictators were the analogues in politics of our soap manufacturer in business. But such men are not so harmful as those who succeed in retaining their power. Any organization, however idealistic its professed aims, may degenerate into a tyranny unless the public firmly retains in its own hands some effective means of controlling leaders. Democracy is the only means so far discovered, but it will not be a completely effective means until it has been broadened and extended to economic regions from which as yet it is excluded. The essential data on this whole subject can only be obtained from a study of history.

The question whether a world State, if established, could be stable, is one belonging to the science of organizations, and is one, therefore, on which history may be expected to throw light. It would be fallacious to argue, as some students of history do, that what never has happened never will happen. Cyrus, in the 6th Century B.C., established an empire of unprecedented magnitude, and was enabled to hold it together by the creation of excellent roads. The Roman Empire, which was still larger, was made possible by even better roads. It is obvious that the aeroplane has, in a much higher degree than the Roman roads, the same effect of making a larger State possible. It is therefore reasonable to expect that it will facilitate the creation of new political forms, and, in particular, that it would enable a world State to be stable if it had a monopoly of air power. There are grave obstacles to the *creation* of a world State, but I do not think it would be difficult to preserve if it once existed.

The question of combining discipline with freedom in the best proportions is one which our age must solve, and solve quickly, if it is to avoid the opposite dangers of anarchy and dictatorship. There has been, ever since

the rise of Greece, an oscillation in this respect, both
in the large and in the small, but an endless see-saw is
surely not the best that human intelligence can com-
pass. What has happened hitherto has been something
like this: a tribe or nation, under a rigid traditional
system, slowly builds up a compressed energy which at
last breaks its bonds; old habits break down first in the
sphere of opinion, and then in the sphere of conduct.
The greatest creative ages are those where opinion is
free, but behavior is still to some extent conventional.
Ultimately, however, skepticism breaks down moral
tabus, society becomes impossibly anarchic, freedom is
succeeded by tyranny, and a new tight tradition is
gradually built up. In Greece, the Homeric heroes
have a fixed pattern of behavior, and a moral code
which even transgressors do not question. In Aeschylus
the old rigidity, somewhat softened, still exists, but the
sophists generated doubt, and Euripides is perplexed
and uncertain. The result, after a period of extraordi-
nary brilliance, was a general decay, first of morals,
and then of other forms of excellence. The rigid
Romans imposed their yoke, but in turn became first
intelligent and then soft. Christianity, more severe
than any previous religion, again created a system in
which the energies of the community were husbanded
but the individual was stifled. In the Italian renaissance
the Christian discipline broke down, to be succeeded
by a brief period of genius and individualism, soon ex-
tinguished by the Spaniards and the counter-reforma-
tion. Similarly the romantic movement led up to the
dictatorships of our own day. The English-speaking
nations, it must be said, have been less subject to these
oscillations than the nations of the Continent of Europe.

The solution of the dilemma between freedom and

discipline must obviously be sought in a compromise. We cannot admire a social system which allows no scope for individual achievement, and we cannot approve one in which excessive individualism makes the social system unstable. Some would argue that there is a fundamental opposition between intelligence and morality, that only stupidity and superstition makes men good, and that an intellectually emancipated man is bound to be completely selfish. This, however, is an obscurantist theory, which takes a wrong view both of morality and of intelligence. Where genuine and superstitious morality have been hopelessly confused in the teaching of the young, it may be difficult for them to disentangle the two. If you have been taught that it is as wicked to swear as it is to steal, you may, when you decide that swearing is permissible, conclude that there is no harm in stealing, but if so that only shows that you are not intelligent and that you were taught a foolish morality. Genuine morality cannot be such as intelligence would undermine, nor does intelligence necessarily promote selfishness. It only does so when unselfishness has been inculcated for the wrong reasons, and then only so long as its purview is limited. In this respect science is a useful element in culture, for it has a stability which intelligence does not shake, and it generates an impersonal habit of mind that makes it natural to accept a social rather than a purely individual ethic. But history is perhaps an even better antidote to anarchic individualism as well as to a lifeless traditionalism.

A few societies have perished from excess of individualism and skepticism; of these Greece and renaissance Italy are the chief examples. These, before perishing, produced a great outburst of genius, from

which the world has profited ever since; they did far
more for mankind than if they had survived in hum-
drum respectability. And their way of perishing is not
the usual way. The usual way is to become sunk in
conservatism, awed by precedent, terrified of novelty,
completely stereotyped in word and deed. Many more
nations have been brought to destruction by fear of
change than by love of it. No nation can long flourish
unless it tolerates exceptional individuals, whose behavior is not exactly like that of their neighbors. Every
one knows that men who achieve great things in art or
literature or science are apt, in youth, to be eccentric;
when eccentricity in youth is not tolerated, there will
be little of great achievement among adult men and
women. But although these things are known, it is
difficult to cause them to be embodied in the practice
of education. It is right that men should live with some
reference to the community, and with some hope of
being useful to it, but this does not mean that all men
should be alike, for exceptional services require exceptional characters.

I have spoken so far of various ways in which history
can be interesting and instructive, but in addition to
these it has a more general function, perhaps more
important than any of them. Our bodily life is confined
to a small portion of time and space, but our mental
life need not be thus limited. What astronomy does to
enlarge the spatial habitat of the mind, history does to
increase its temporal domain. Our private lives are
often exasperating, and sometimes almost intolerably
painful. To see them in perspective, as an infinitesimal
fragment in the life of mankind, makes it less difficult
to endure personal evils which cannot be evaded. Although history is full of ups and downs, there is a gen-

eral trend in which it is possible to feel some satisfaction; we know more than our ancestors knew, we have more command over the forces of nature, we suffer less from disease and from natural cataclysms. It is true that we have not yet learnt to protect ourselves from each other: man is as dangerous to man as he ever was. But even in this respect there are at least the preliminaries of improvement. Violence now is mainly organized and governmental, and it is easier to imagine ways of ending this than of ending the sporadic unplanned violence of more primitive times.

The perspective of history enables us to see more clearly what events and what sorts of activities have permanent importance. Most of the contemporaries of Galileo saw far more significance in the Thirty Years' War than in his discoveries, but to us it is evident that the war was a 30 years' futility, while his discoveries began a new era. When Gladstone visited Darwin, Darwin observed afterwards: "What an honor to be visited by so great a man." His modesty was amiable, but showed a lack of historical perspective. Many occurrences—party contests, for example—rouse at the time an excitement quite out of proportion to their real importance, whereas the greatest events, like the summits of high mountains, though dominant from far away, are screened by the foreground from a nearer view. It is a help towards sanity and calm judgment to acquire the habit of seeing contemporary events in their historical setting, and of imagining them as they will appear when they are in the past. Theologians assure us that God sees all time as though it were present; it is not in human power to do this except to a very limited degree, but in so far as we can do it, it is a help towards wisdom and contemplative insight. We live in the present, and in the present we must act; but life is not all action, and action is best when it proceeds from a wide survey in which the present loses the sharpness of its emotional insistence. Men are born and die; some leave hardly a trace, others transmit something of good or evil to future ages. The man whose thoughts and feelings are enlarged by history will wish to be a transmitter, and to transmit, so far as may be, what his successors will judge to have been good.

The Value of Free Thought

The expression "free thought" is often used as if it meant merely opposition to the prevailing orthodoxy. But this is only a symptom of free thought, frequent, but invariable. "Free thought" means thinking freely —as freely, at least, as is possible for a human being. The person who is free in any respect if free *from* something; what is the free thinker free from? To be worthy of the name, he must be free of two things: the force of tradition, and the tyranny of his own passions. No one is *completely* free from either, but in the measure of a man's emancipation he deserves to be called a free thinker. A man is not to be denied this title because he happens, on some point, to agree with the theologians of his country. An Arab who, starting from the first principles of human reason, is able to deduce that the Koran was not created, but existed eternally in heaven, may be counted as a free thinker, provided he is willing to listen to counter arguments and subject his ratiocination to critical scrutiny. On the same conditions, a European who, from a definition of benevolence, is able to show that a benevolent Deity will subject infants to an eternity of torment if they die before some one sprinkles them with water to the accompaniment of certain magical words, will have to be regarded as satisfying our definition. What makes a free thinker is not his beliefs, but the way in which he holds

them. If he holds them because his elders told him
they were true when he was young, or if he holds them
because if he did not he would be unhappy, his thought
is not free; but if he holds them because, after careful
thought, he finds a balance of evidence in their favor,
then his thought is free, however odd his conclusions
may seem.

Freedom from the tyranny of passion is as essential
as freedom from the influence of tradition. The lunatic
who thinks he is God or the governor of the Bank of
England is not a free thinker, because he has allowed
the passion of megalomania to get the better of his
reason. The jealous husband, who suspects his wife
of infidelity on inadequate grounds, and the complacent optimist, who refuses to suspect her when the
evidence is overwhelming, are alike permitting passion to enslave their thought; in neither of them is
thought free.

The freedom that the freethinker seeks is not the
absolute freedom of anarchy; it is freedom within the
intellectual law. He will not bow to the authority of
others, and he will not bow to his own desires, but he
will submit to evidence. Prove to him that he is mistaken, and he will change his opinion; supply him with
a new fact, and he will if necessary abandon even his
most cherished theories. This is not to him a slavery,
since his desire is to *know,* not to indulge in pretty fan-
cies. The desire for knowledge has an element of humility towards facts; in opinion, it submits to the universe. But towards mankind it is not humble; it will
not accept as genuine knowledge the counterfeit coin
that is too often offered with all the apparatus of authority. The free thinker knows that to control his
environment he must understand it, and that the illu-

sion of power to be derived from myths is no better than that of a boastful drunkard. He needs, towards his fellow men, independence; towards his own prejudices, a difficult self-discipline; and towards the world that he wishes to understand a clear untroubled outlook which endeavors to see without distortion.

Is the free thinker, as we have been describing him, a desirable member of society, or is he a menace to all that we ought to hold sacred? In almost all times and places, he has been held to be a menace, and he is still held to be so, in varying degrees, in almost every country. In Germany he is sent to a concentration camp, in Russia to a Labor Colony in the Arctic; in Japan he is imprisoned for "dangerous thoughts"; in the United States, though not subject to legal penalties, he is debarred from teaching in the great majority of schools and universities, and has no chance of a political career. Throughout a period of about 1,200 years, every Christian country in Europe condemned free thinkers to be burnt at the stake. In Mohammedan countries, though often protected by monarchs, they were subjects of abhorrence to the mob even in the greatest periods of Arabic and Moorish culture. A hostility so widespread and so nearly universal must have deep roots, partly in human nature, partly in the statecraft of governing cliques; in either case, the soil in which they flourish is fear.

Let us consider some of the arguments against free thought that are used by those who are not content with a mere appeal to prejudice.

There is first the appeal to modesty, which is used especially by the old in dealing with rebellious youth. Wise men throughout the ages, it is said, have all been agreed in upholding certain great truths, and who are you to set yourself up against their unanimous testimony? If you are prepared to reject St. Paul and St. Augustine will you be equally contemptuous of Plato and Aristotle? Or, if you despise all the ancients, what about Descartes and Spinoza, Kant and Hegel? Were they not great intellects, who probed matters more deeply than you can hope to do? And is not the pastor of your parents' church a virtuous and learned man, who has a degree in theology, and even spent some months in the study of Hebrew? Have you forgotten what Bacon, that good and great man, said about a *little* knowledge inclining to atheism? Do you pretend that there are no mysteries before which the human intellect is dumb? Pride of intellect is a sin, and you commit it when you set up your own judgment against that of all the wisest men of many centuries.

This argument, expressed in Latin—which is held to make any nonsense respectable—has been erected by the Catholic Church into a first principle: that we cannot err in believing what has been believed always, everywhere, and by everybody. Those who use this argument conveniently forget how many once universal beliefs are now discarded. It was held that there could not be men at the antipodes, because they would fall off, or at least grow dizzy from standing upside down. Everybody believed that the sun goes round the earth, that there are unicorns, and that toads are poisonous. Until the 16th Century, no one questioned the efficacy of witchcraft; of those who first doubted the truth of this superstition, not a few were burnt at the stake. Who now accepts the doctrine, once almost universal throughout Christendom, that infants who die without being baptized will spend eternity in hell because Adam ate an apple? Yet all these now obsolete doctrines could formerly have been upheld by the appeal to the wisdom of the ages.

The appeal to authority is fallacious, but even so it is questionable whether, if admitted, it would work more in favor of Christianity than against it. I have spent most of my life in the society of authors and men of science; among them, free thought is taken for granted, and the few exceptions are noted as freaks. It is true that most of them have too much worldly wisdom to allow their opinions to become known to the orthodox, for even now a *known* freethinker suffers various disabilities, and has much more difficulty in making a living than a man who is reputed to accept the teachings of some Church. It is only by imposing this somewhat flimsy hypocrisy that believers are still able to deceive the young by appealing to authority.

The study of anthropology is useful in this respect. Savages at a certain stage of development are found to have very similar beliefs in all parts of the world, and to the modern mind these beliefs are almost all absurd. But if mankind continues to advance, we shall, 20,000 years hence, appear to our successors scarcely distinguishable from the savages to whom we feel ourselves so superior. It is customary to date anthropological epochs by the materials employed—the stone age, the bronze age, the iron age. But one might equally describe a culture by its prevalent beliefs: the cannibal culture, the animal sacrifice culture, the transubstantiation culture, and so on into the future. To see our beliefs as one stage in this development is wholesome. It shows that there is nothing which has been believed "always, everywhere, and by everybody"; and that

whatever has been believed by everybody in a certain
stage of culture has seemed nonsense to everybody in
the next stage.

The common body of wisdom to which the conventional and orthodox like to appeal is a myth; there is
only the "wisdom" of one time and place. In every age
and in every place, if you wish to be thought well of
by influential citizens you must at least seem to share
their prejudices, and you must close your mind to the
fact that influential citizens in other times and places
have quite different prejudices. If, on the other hand,
you wish to acquire knowledge, you must ignore the
influential citizens, and rely upon your judgment, even
when you accept the authority of those whom your
own judgment pronounces worthy of respect. This
degree of reliance upon yourself is the first step towards freedom of thought. Not that you need think
yourself infallible, but that you must learn to think
every one fallible, and to content yourself with such
greater or less probability as the evidence may seem to
you to warrant. This renunciation of absolute certainty
is, to some minds, the most difficult step towards intellectual freedom.

Of all the arguments designed to show that free
thought is wicked, the one most often used is that without religion people would not be virtuous. Their virtue,
we are told, will fail for two reasons, first, that they will
no longer fear personal punishment, and second, that
they will no longer know what is virtue and what is
sin. In using this argument, orthodox Catholics have
in some ways a logical advantage over Protestants. Let
us see how the argument looks from a Catholic point
of view.

The theology of sin has always been somewhat intricate, since it has had to face the fundamental question: why did God permit sin? St. Augustine held that, from the moment when Adam ate the apple, men have not had free will; they could not, by their own efforts, abstain from sin. Since sin deserves punishment, God would have been entirely just if He had condemned the whole human race to hell. But mercy is also a virtue, and in order to exercise this virtue He had to send another portion of the human race to heaven. Nothing but pure caprice, St. Augustine maintained, determined His choice of the elect and the reprobate. But on the elect, when He had chosen them, He bestowed grace, so that they were able, within limits, to abstain from sin. They were virtuous because they were saved, not saved because they were virtuous. For some obscure reason, grace was never bestowed on the unbaptized.

A certain kindly Welshman named Morgan, who translated his name into Pelagius, was a contemporary of St. Augustine, and combated his doctrine as too severe. Pelagius held that men still have free will, in spite of Adam's sin. He thought it even possible that a human being might be entirely without sin. He thought that the wicked are damned because they sin, whereas St. Augustine thought that they sin because they are damned. Pelagius held that each man had the power to live so virtuously as to deserve heaven, and that his use of his own free will determined the issue between salvation and damnation. St. Augustine's authority secured the condemnation of this doctrine, which remained heretical until the Reformation. But at the Reformation Luther and Calvin espoused the theory of predestination with such ardor that the Catholic Church, without formal change, turned increasingly towards the doctrine of Pelagius. This doctrine is now held, in practice if not in theory, not only by the Catholic Church, but also by the great majority of the Protestants. It has, however, been still further softened by the belief that fewer people go to hell than was formerly thought. Indeed, among Protestants, a complete rejection of hell has become very common.

A belief in either hell or purgatory ought, one would suppose, to have a powerful influence in promoting whatever the theologians consider to be virtue. If you accept St. Augustine's doctrine, you will hold that, although it is not virtue that causes you to go to heaven, virtue is a *mark* of the elect; if you live a sinful life, you will be forced to conclude that you are among the reprobate. You will therefore live virtuously in order to hope that you will go to heaven. If you accept the more usual view that you will be punished hereafter for your sins, either by spending eternity in hell or by a longer or shorter period of purgatorial fires, you will, if you are prudent, consider that, on the balance, the virtuous enjoy more pleasure than the wicked, and that therefore, as a rational hedonist, you had better abstain from sin. If, on the other hand, you do not believe in the life hereafter, you will sin whenever no earthly penalty is to be feared—so at least orthodox theologians seem to think. Whether from introspection or for some other reason, they seem to be all agreed that *disinterested* virtue is impossible.

However that may be, the views of the early Church on sin were found to be too severe for ordinary human nature, and were softened in various ways which, incidentally, increased the power of the priesthood. The sacrament of absolution secures sinners against the

extreme penalty of damnation; you may commit all
the sins you have a mind to, provided you repent on
your deathbed and receive extreme unction. True, you
may suffer for a while in purgatory, but your sojourn
there can be shortened if masses are said for your soul,
and priests will say masses for you if you leave them
money for the purpose. Thus the power of wealth ex-
tends beyond the grave, and bribery is effective even
in heaven. This comfortable doctrine left the rich and
powerful free to indulge their passions as they saw fit.
In the ages of faith, murder and rape were far com-
moner than they have since become. The supposed
efficacy of orthodox belief in curbing sin is not borne
out by history. Not only have believers been prone to
sin, but unbelievers have often been exceptionally virtuous; it would be difficult to point to any set of men
more impeccable than the earnest free thinkers of the
19th Century.

But, the champion of orthodoxy will object, when
freethinkers are virtuous, it is because they live in a
Christian community and have imbibed its ethic in
youth; without this influence, they would question the
moral law and see no reason to abstain from any in-
famy. The sins of the Nazis and the Bolsheviks are
pointed out as the fruits of free thought. But they are
not freethinkers according to our definition: they are
fanatical adherents of absurd creeds, and their crimes
spring from their fanaticism. They are, in fact, the
same crimes as those committed by men like Charles
V or Philip II, who were champions of the faith.
Charles V, after spending the day conquering a Protestant city, felt that he had earned a little relaxation;
he sent his servants out to find a virgin, and they found

one of 17. Presumably she got syphilis, but the Emperor got absolution. This is the system which is supposed to preserve men from sin.

On the other hand, many who are now universally acknowledged to have been quite exceptionally virtuous incurred obloquy, if not worse, for their opposition to the orthodoxy of their day. Socrates, on the ground that he was guilty of impiety, was condemned to drink the hemlock. Giordano Bruno was burnt by the Inquisition and Servetus was burnt by Calvin, both because, though men of the highest moral excellence, they had fallen into heresy. Spinoza, one of the noblest men known to history, was excommunicated by the Jews and execrated by the Christians; for a hundred years after his death, hardly any one dared to say a good word for him. The English and American freethinkers of the 18th and early 19th centuries were, for the most part, men of quite exceptional moral excellence; in some cases, such as the Founding Fathers, this is so evident that the orthodox have been driven to conceal the fact that men so universally admired had shocking opinions. In our day free thought still leads men into trouble, but less for attacks on dogma than for criticism of the superstitious parts of religious ethics.

There are, it is true, some actions labelled "sin" which are likely to be promoted by free thought. A Jew, when he ceases to be orthodox, may eat pork; a Hindu may commit the offense of eating beef. The Greek Orthodox Church considers it sin for godparents of the same child to marry; I will not deny that free thought may encourage this enormity. Protestants condemn amusements on Sunday, and Catholics condemn birth control; in these respects, also, free thought may be inimical to what bigots choose to call virtue. Moral codes which are irrational, and have no basis except in superstition, cannot long survive the habit of disinterested thinking. But if a moral code seems to promote human well-being in this terrestrial existence, it has no need of supernatural sanctions. Kindliness and intelligence are the chief sources of useful behavior, and neither is promoted by causing people to believe, against all reason, in a capricious and vindictive deity who practices a degree of cruelty which, in the strictest mathematic sense, surpasses infinitely that of the worst human beings who have ever existed. Modern liberal Christians may protest that this is not the sort of God in whom they believe, but they should realize that only the teachings of persecuted freethinkers have caused this moral advance in their beliefs.

I come now to another class of arguments against free thought, namely those which may be called political. In former times, these arguments took a very crude form: it is all very well (it was said) for the rich and powerful to be skeptics, but the poor need some theological belief to make them contented with their lot. If they can be induced to think that this life of tribulation is only a brief prelude to eternal bliss, and that rewards in heaven are much more likely to go to the poor than to the rich, they will be less inclined to listen to subversive propaganda, particularly if heaven is only to be the reward of the submissive. This point of view existed in antiquity and throughout the Middle Ages, but it was especially prevalent in the early 19th Century, when the preaching of Methodism induced acquiescence among the victims of the atrocious industrial system of that period. This frank defense of earthly injustice as a preface to celestial justice has

now been pretty generally abandoned, but not, for the
most part, through the initiative of champions of religion. It was mainly men like Tom Paine, Robert
Owen, and Karl Marx, freethinkers all, who shamed
the orthodox rich out of this complacent attempt to
interpret God as the Supreme Capitalist.

There is, however, a generalized form of the same
argument, which deserves more respect, and calls for
serious discussion. In this form, the argument main-
tains that social cohesion, without which no community can survive, is only rendered possible by some
unifying creed or moral code, and that no such creed
or code can long survive the corrosive effect of skeptical criticism. There have been periods—so it is alleged
—when denial of traditional orthodoxies caused political disaster; of these the most notable are the great age
of Greece and the epoch of the Italian Renaissance. It
is customary among the ignorant to bring up the fall
of Rome in this connection, and to link it with the
wickedness of Nero. But as the fall of Rome did not
occur until 400 years after the time of Nero, and as
meanwhile the Romans had undergone a great moral
purification, culminating in the adoption of Christianity, this example is ill chosen. The other two deserve
more serious discussion.

The Greek cities lost their independence, first to the
Macedonians, and then, more completely, to the
Romans, and this loss occurred at a time when the
ancient pieties had been dissolved by free inquiry. But
there is no reason to connect their fall with their skepticism. They fell because they could not unite, and
their failure to unite was due to ordinary political
causes, such as, in our own day, prevented the smaller
neutrals from uniting against Hitler. No intensity of

religious belief could have saved them; only a rare degree of political sagacity would have been of any service. Carthage fell equally, though at the crisis the Carthaginians sacrificed their children to Moloch as religiously as any champion of religion could wish.

Much the same considerations apply to Italy in the renaissance. France and Spain were Great Powers, to which the small Italian States could offer no effective opposition. In the face of traditional enmities unity was difficult, as it always is in such circumstances; its most forceful advocate was the wicked Machievelli, and, as he points out, its most powerful opponent was the Pope. No serious historical student can maintain that the enslavement of Italy was due to lack of religion.

We may however concede one thing to those who urge that religion is socially necessary. Where the Church has been a very powerful organization, and has played a great part in regulating men's lives, its sudden dissolution may leave them without the accustomed external guidance, and render society somewhat chaotic until new organizations grow up. But in this respect the Church is no different from any other important organization. Social cohesion is important, and the Church has been one of the ways of securing it, but there are innumerable other ways which do not demand so high a price in mental bondage.

Some men argue that the question whether religious dogmas are true or false is unimportant; the important thing, they say, is that these beliefs are comforting. How could we face life, they ask, if this world were all, and if we had no assurance that its apparent evil serves some great purpose? Will not belief in immortality promote courage in the face of death? Will not the belief that the course of history is ordained by an all-wise beneficent Providence help us to stand firm in times when evil appears to be triumphant? Why rob ourselves or others of this source of happiness by listening to the dubious arguments of those who refuse to believe in anything that cannot be demonstrated by the cold intellect? Has not the heart its rights? Why should it submit to the head? As the poet Tennyson exclaims in rebutting the contentions of skeptics:

> Like a man in wrath the heart
> Stood up and answered: I have felt.

There is to my mind something pusillanimous and sniveling about this point of view, which makes me scarcely able to consider it with patience. To refuse to face facts merely because they are unpleasant is considered the mark of a weak character, except in the sphere of religion. I do not see how it can be ignoble to yield to the tyranny of fear in all ordinary terrestrial matters, but noble and virtuous to do exactly the same thing when God and the future life are concerned.

But, the defenders of orthodoxy may argue, you do not *know* that religious beliefs are untrue. Where all is doubtful, why not accept the more cheerful alternative? This is the argument of William James's "Will to Believe." The duty of veracity, he says, has two parts: first, to believe what is true; second, to disbelieve what is false. To these two parts he attaches equal authority. The skeptic, who suspends judgment in the absence of adequate evidence, is certainly failing to believe what is true, whereas, if he adopted either alternative, he *might* be succeeding in believing what is true. On this ground, in the name of veracity, William James condemns the skeptic.

His argument, however, is shockingly sophistical. The virtue of veracity does not consist in believing all sorts of things at a venture, on the off chance that they may happen to be true. No one would for a moment take this point of view except as regards religion. Suppose I get into conversation with a stranger, am I to believe that his name is Wilkinson on the ground that, if it is, I shall be believing truly, whereas if I admit that I do not yet know his name I forfeit the chance of a true belief? You will say that there are known to be many surnames, and therefore each is improbable. But there are also many religions. If I am to believe at a venture, shall I believe what I am told by the Buddhists, or the Hindus, or the Christians? And if I choose the Christians, shall I prefer the Catholics, or the Lutherans, or the Calvinists, or the Muggletonians, or the Particular Baptists? On William James' principle I ought to believe them all, so as to have the greatest possible chance of believing something true.

The inconclusive character of the arguments *against* this or that theological dogma, even when fully admitted, does not justify belief in any one of the mutually inconsistent systems that human fantasy has created. I cannot *prove* that the Hindus are mistaken in attributing a peculiar sacredness to the cow, or that the Mohammedans are wrong in thinking that only the followers of the Prophet will enjoy the delights of paradise. Perhaps Mr. Muggleton was as great a man as the Muggletonians contend; perhaps the Seventh Day Adventists are right in thinking that it is on Saturdays that God wants us to do no work. But if we are going to adopt all these beliefs, as William James's principles would lead us to do, we shall find life somewhat difficult. We must not eat beef because the Hindus may be right, or pork because the Jews may be right, or beans because Pythagoras forbade them. We must not work on Fridays, Saturdays, or Sundays, to obey Mohammedan, Jewish and Christian precepts; the remaining days will mostly be sacred days in some religion. Perhaps in the end a general skepticism may seem less inconvenient than the consolations of all the religions at once. But how is a fair-minded man to choose among them?

The virtue of veracity, as I conceive it, consists in giving to every suggested belief the degree of credence that the evidence warrants. We give whole-hearted credence to our perceptions, almost complete credence to what is well-established in science, such as predictions of eclipses, but much less to what is still somewhat tentative, such as the weather forecast. We do not doubt that there was a famous man called Julius Caesar, but about Zoroaster we are not so sure. Veracity does not consist simply in believing or disbelieving, but also in suspending judgment, and in thinking some things probable and others improbable.

But, says William James, you must in any doubtful situation, act either on belief or disbelief, and whichever you act upon the other alternative is practically rejected. This is an undue simplification. Many hypotheses are worth acting upon in certain ways, but not in others. If I am healthy, I may act upon the hypothesis that the weather is going to be fine, but if I have a peculiar sensibility to chills I may require very strong evidence before it becomes wise to adopt this hypothesis. I may act upon the hypothesis that only the good can go to heaven to the extent of being good myself, without being justified in acting on it to the extent of burning those whom I think not good.

We are all obliged constantly to act upon doubtful hypotheses, but when we do so we ought to take care that the results will not be very disastrous if the hypotheses are false. And when we act upon a doubtful hypothesis, we ought not to persuade ourselves that it is certain, for then we close our minds against new evidence, and also venture on actions (such as persecution) which are very undesirable if the hypothesis is false. And for this reason praise and blame ought not to be attached to beliefs or disbeliefs, but only to rational or irrational ways of holding them.

The importance of free thought is the same thing as the importance of veracity. Veracity does not necessarily consist in believing what is in fact true, because sometimes the available evidence may point to a wrong conclusion. Occasions may arise when the most conscientious jury will condemn a man who is in fact innocent, because unfortunate circumstances have made him seem guilty. To be always right is not possible for human beings, but it is possible always to *try* to be right. Veracity consists in trying to be right in matters of belief, and also in doing what is possible to insure that others are right.

Why should veracity be regarded as important? The reasons are partly personal, partly social. Let us begin with the social reasons.

Every powerful individual or group depends upon the existence of certain beliefs in others. The Dalai Lama is powerful in Tibet, the Caliph used to be powerful in the Muslim world, the Pope is powerful among Catholics, and the power of these men depends upon the belief of their followers that they have some peculiar holiness. The Dalai Lama makes (or made) large sums of money by selling pills made out of his excrement. What the Caliph used to make out of being holy is familiar to every reader of the Arabian Nights. The Pope has been shorn of some of his glory by the wickedness of Protestants and freethinkers, but in the great days of the Italian renaissance he enjoyed immense splendor. Is it to be supposed that men in such a position will encourage a rational examination of their claims? The Dalai Lama, like the vendors of patent medicines among ourselves, would obviously stick at nothing to prevent a scientific investigation of the efficacy of various pills, or at any rate to prevent its results from becoming known. He may himself, like some of the Renaissance Popes, be completely skeptical, but he will not wish his disciples to resemble him in this respect.

Wherever there is power, there is a temptation to encourage irrational credulity in those who are subject to the power in question. Kings have been supposed to be sacred beings; the Mikado is still a divinity descended from the sun-goddess. Sometimes the business of sacredness is overdone. The king of Dahomey had such majesty that whenever he looked towards any part of his dominions tempests arose in that part; he therefore had to look always at the ground, which made him easy to assassinate. But when the king as an individual is hampered in this way, certain people in his entourage can use his magical powers for their own ends, so that there is no gain to the public.

When superstition is needed to promote tyranny, free thought is likely to cause revolution. But when the population has been accustomed to irrational reverence, it is likely to transfer its reverence to the leader of a successful revolution. Ikons are still habitual in Russia, but of Lenin or Stalin instead of Our Lady. The chief gain in such a case is that the new superstition is not likely to have such a firm hold as the old one had; Stalin-worship could be upset by a less terrific upheaval than the revolution of 1917.

If a population is to escape tyranny, it must have a free-thinking attitude towards its government and the theories upon which its government is based, that is to say, it must demand that the government shall act in the general interest, and must not be deceived by a superstitious theology into the belief that what is in fact only the interest of the governing clique is identical with the general interest. For obedience to a tolerable government there are abundant rational motives, but when obedience is given for irrational reasons the resulting slavishness encourages the government to become tyrannical.

Ever since the Reformation, the State has increasingly replaced the Church as the object of superstitious reverence. At first, the State was embodied in the King: Henry VIII in England and Louis XIV in France were able to do abominable things because of the divinity that doth hedge a king. But in Germany and Russia it has been found possible, by means of a fanatical creed, to generate a similar feeling of awe towards a revolutionary leader, and in order to achieve this end free thought has been suppressed more vigorously than at any time since the 17th Century. Only a general growth of free thought can, in the long run, save these countries from a self-imposed despotism.

The use of control over opinion to promote the power of a dominant class is best shown in the growth

of Catholic theology. The power of the priesthood
depends upon its ability to decide whether you shall
go to heaven or to hell, and, in the former event, how
long you shall spend in purgatory. What must you do
in order to be among the fortunate? Must you lead
a virtuous life? Must you love your neighbor, as Christ
ordained? Or must you obey the still more difficult
precept to sell all you have and give to the poor? No,
you need do none of these things. Getting to heaven
is a matter of red tape, like getting to a foreign country in war time.

First, you must avoid heresy, that is to say, you must
believe everything that the Church tells you to believe.
You need not know what the dogmas of the Church
are, because that is difficult except for educated theologians, but you must hold no opinions contrary to
these dogmas, and, if you ever feel tempted to do so,
you must abandon the dangerous opinions as soon as
you are officially informed that they are not orthodox.
In a word, on all the most important subjects you must
never think for yourself.

As regards conduct, you need not avoid sin; indeed,
it is heretical to suppose that you can. You are sure to
sin, but that need not trouble you provided you take
the proper steps. There are seven deadly sins; if you
commit any of these, and die before taking the proper
steps, you will go to hell, but all can be forgiven to
those who go through the correct routine. You must
first tell some priest all about it, and profess due pen-
itence. He can then absolve you, but may impose a
penance as the condition of absolution. You are now
safe from hell, so far as that particular sin is concerned,
but to shorten your time in purgatory there are various
things that it is wise to do, most of which increase

either the power or the income of the priesthood. If you have enough money, you can commit a great many sins and nevertheless get to heaven pretty soon. The more sins you commit, the more the Church profits by the steps you have to take to mitigate the punishment. The system is convenient both for priests and for sinners, but it is preposterous to pretend that it promotes virtue. What it does promote is mental docility and abject fear.

I do not wish to suggest that these defects are peculiarly characteristic of the Catholic Church. They exist equally under the tyranny of the Nazi party and the Communist party. The sins to which these parties object are somewhat different from those to which the Church objects: in particular, they are less obsessed by sex. And the punishment of sin, under their regime, is in this world, not in the next. But otherwise there is much similarity, except for the differences that must exist between what is new and what is old and tried and established. What is in common is the power of one group, based on irrational beliefs. And the ultimate cure, in all these forms of mental tyranny, is freedom of thought.

It is odd that the orthodox, while decrying free thought in their own day, are quite willing to admit a host of truths which would never have become known but for the freethinkers of earlier ages. It was freethinkers in early Greece who persuaded their compatriots, in spite of the opposition of the priests of Delphi, to abandon the practice of human sacrifice. Anaxagoras, who taught that the sun and moon are not gods, only escaped death for impiety by flight from Athens. Those who disbelieved in witchcraft were told, quite truly, that to question witchcraft is to question the Bible. Galileo, for holding that the earth goes round the sun, was forced under threat of torture to recant, was kept in prison, and was ordered to repeat daily the seven penitential psalms to show his contrition for having used his mind. Darwin, fortunately for himself, lived in an age when persecution was in abeyance, but he was denounced by the orthodox, and they would have suppressed his teaching if they had had the power. Every intellectual advance, and a great many moral reforms, have had to fight for victory against the forces of obscurantism. Nevertheless, in what the obscurantists still defend, they are as obstinate as they ever were. Progress, now as in the past, is only possible in the teeth of their bitter hostility.

The personal and private reasons in favor of veracity in thinking are no less cogent than the public reasons. We all know the kind of person who cannot bear any unpalatable fact, and we know that, to those who live with them, they appear irritating and contemptible. In Shakespeare's "Antony and Cleopatra" Cleopatra orders the messenger who brings news of Antony's marriage to Octavia to be scourged. After this, people are wary of telling her anything that may annoy her, and, hugging her illusions, she goes straight to disaster. In regard to mundane affairs, the capacity to assimilate what is unpleasant is a condition of success, and for this reason, if for no other, it is a mistake to wrap oneself around with comfortable fairy-tales.

But, it will be said, beliefs about the next world are in quite a different category. However false they may be, they will not be refuted by any experience during this life. Even if there is no such place as heaven, the man who expects to go there will have a happier life than the man who regards death as annihilation. What advantage is there, then, in thinking truly about such a matter?

Now to begin with, veracity consists, as we have already said, not in having true beliefs, but in trying to have them. The man who, after a dispassionate examination of the evidence, has decided that there is a future life, is not lacking in veracity; this lack exists only in the believer who refuses to examine the evidence because he fears that it may prove inadequate. This man is like one who refuses to open a letter because it may contain bad news. When a man allows one kind of fear to dominate him, he soon comes to be dominated by other kinds also. The world in which we live is full of unpleasant things, some of which are pretty sure to happen to ourselves. If we are to preserve self-respect, and to merit the respect of others, we must learn to endure such things, not only when they happen, but in prospect. The man who fears that there is no evidence for immortality, but nevertheless clings to the belief by closing his mind, is no better than a man who fears he has cancer, but refuses a medical examination lest his fears should be confirmed. Each alike is on a level with the soldier who runs away in battle.

One of the worst aspects of orthodox Christianity is that it sanctifies fear, both personal and impersonal. Fear of hell, fear of extinction, fear lest the universe should be purposeless, are regarded as noble emotions, and men who allow themselves to be dominated by such fears are thought superior to men who face what is painful without flinching. But human nature cannot be so completely departmentalized that fear can be exalted in one direction without acquiring a hold in other directions also. The man who thinks himself

virtuous in fearing an angry God will soon begin to
see virtue in submission to earthly tyrants. In the best
character there is an element of pride—not the sort of
pride that despises others, but the sort that will not be
deflected from what it thinks good by outside pressure.
The man who has this sort of pride will wish, as far
as may be, to know the truth about matters that con-
cern him, and will feel himself a slave if, in his thought,
he yields to fear. But this kind of pride is condemned
by the Church as a sin, and is called "pride of intellect." For my part, so far from regarding it as a sin, I
hold it to be one of the greatest and most desirable of
virtues.

But it is time to tackle the more specific questions:
Is there evidence in favor of Christian dogmas, either
in the old rigid forms or in the vaguer forms favored
by modernists? And, if there is not such evidence, is
there nevertheless reason to think that belief in Christian dogmas does good?

The old orthodoxy has now fallen into almost universal disfavor, even among Catholics. Catholics still
believe in hell, but by means of the doctrine of invin-
cible ignorance they escape the necessity of believing
that their Protestant friends will go there. Indeed there
is hardly anybody they know to be damned, except
Judas Iscariot. Nevertheless, they are still, theoretically,
in favor of persecution, of which the justification was
that heresy leads to damnation. In this as in various
other respects, Catholic ethics has not yet drawn all
the inferences that follow from the liberalizing of Catholic theology. Perhaps in time these inferences will be
drawn. But as in purely theological matters, the driv-
ing force will have to come from freethinkers. But

for their influence, Catholic theology would still be as rigid as in the middle ages.

I think we may say that what is essential to Christianity as conceived by modern theologians is belief in God and immortality, together with a moral code which is more traditional than that of most freethinkers.

What reasons are there for belief in God? In old days, there were a variety of purely intellectual arguments, which were thought to make it irrational to doubt the existence of God. The chief of these was the argument of the First Cause: in tracing events backward from effects to causes, we must, it was thought, come to an end somewhere, since an infinite series is impossible. Wherever we come to an end, we have reached a Cause which is not an effect, and this Cause is God. This and other purely intellectual arguments were criticized by freethinkers, and in the end most theologians came to admit that they are invalid. The arguments upon which most modern theologians rely are less precise and more concerned with moral issues. In the main, they result from examination of what is called the religious consciousness or the religious experience. I do not think they are any more cogent than the old arguments, but because of their vagueness they are less susceptible to precise refutations.

We are told that we have a moral sense which must have had a supernatural origin. We are told also that certain people have religious experiences in which they become aware of God with the same certainty with which we become aware of tables and chairs. It is thought to be irrational to question this evidence merely on the ground that only certain people have the mystical experiences in question. We accept a host of things in science on the word of certain skilled observers; why not accept things in religion on the word of the skilled observers in this field?

To the mystic, who is persuaded that he himself has seen God, it is useless to argue about the matter. If he has moments when he is amenable to reason, one may point out that innumerable people have seen Satan, in whom most modern mystics do not believe. We may point out that Mr. So-and-So, who is a devotee of the worship of Bacchus, has seen pink rats, but has not been able to persuade other zoologists of their reality. We may trace the history of visions and hallucinations, pointing out how they are colored by the previous beliefs of the seers or lunatics concerned. St. Anthony in the desert was constantly troubled by apparitions of naked ladies; are we to infer that the Koran is right in promising abundance of such sights in Paradise? Perish the thought!

Such things, I say, we may point out, but probably in vain. A lady of my acquaintance took to fasting, and recommended the practice on the ground that it gave rise to visions. "Yes," I said, "if you drink too much you see snakes, and if you eat too little you see angels." But, alas! she was only annoyed. She held, as many mystics do, that a vision must be veridical if it is edifying and results from virtuous living. This view is only justified if we already know that the world is governed by a beneficent Providence which rewards those who obey its laws by allowing them glimpses of the felicity to come. What if, as some heretics have thought, this world is the empire of Satan, who rewards the wicked not only with riches and power, but with hidden magical lore? In that case, the visions of the wicked will deserve more credence than those of the good, and we shall listen with more respect to the revelations of the drunkard than to those of the ascetic. Before we can decide, therefore, what weight to attach to the testimony of the mystics, we must first inquire whether there are any grounds for believing in a good God.

God, in orthodox theology, is the omnipotent Creator, who made the world out of nothing. There are some liberal theologians nowadays who deny His omnipotence; I shall consider their view presently, but first let us examine the more usual and correct opinion.

This view has been most clearly and exactly expressed by the philosopher Leibniz. According to him, God, before creating the world, surveyed all the worlds that are logically possible, and compared them as the amount of good and evil that they severally contained. Being beneficent, He decided to create that one of the possible worlds that contained the greatest excess of good over evil. This world happened to contain a good deal of evil, but the evil was logically bound up with the greater good. In particular, sin is an evil, but free will is a good. Not even omnipotence can confer free will without the possibility of sin, but free will is so great a good that God decided to create a world containing both free will and sin rather than a world containing neither. He did so, and Adam ate the apple. Hence all our sorrows.

This is a pretty fable, and I will not deny that it is logically possible, but that is the utmost that I will concede. It is exactly equally possible that the world

was created by a wholly malicious devil, who allowed
a certain amount of good in order to increase the sum
of evil. Let us suppose his ethical valuations to be entirely orthodox, but his will to be towards what is bad.
He would agree with the theologians in thinking sin
the greatest of evils, and would perceive that sin is
impossible without free will. He would therefore create things possessed of free will, in spite of the fact
that free will made virtue possible. He would be con-
soled, however, by the foreknowledge that virtue
would be very rare. And so this actual world, which
he created, is the worst of all possible worlds, although
it contains some things that are good.

I am not advocating this fable, any more than Leibniz's. Both seem to me to be equally fantastic. The
only difference between them is that one is pleasant,
the other unpleasant, but this difference has sufficed
to make Christians accept the one and reject the other.
No one asked: Why should the truth be pleasant?
What reason have we to think our wishes a key to
reality? the only rational answer is: None whatever.

The shifts to which theologians have been put to
prove the world such as a good God could have created are sometimes very curious. In 1755 there was a
great earthquake in Lisbon, which shook Voltaire's
faith. But Rousseau pointed out that the loss of life
was due to people living in high houses; if they had
run wild in the woods, like the noble savage, they
would not have suffered; they were therefore justly
punished for their sins. Bernard Bosanquet, the leading
British philosopher of my youth, went so far as to argue that, on purely logical grounds, earthquakes,
though possible in second-rate capitals such as Lisbon,
could not occur in a really great city like London. The

Tokyo earthquake occurred after his book was published, but then the Japanese, as we know, are wicked.

In the 18th Century it was held that all suffering, even that of animals, is due to Adam's sin, and did not exist before the fall. Until that fatal moment, mosquitoes did not sting, snakes were not venomous, and lions were strictly vegetarian. Unfortunately, in the early 19th Century geologists discovered fossils of carnivorous animals which, it was rightly held, must have existed before man appeared on the earth. We can all see how right and just it is that animals eaten by other animals should suffer because Adam and Eve were wicked, but why should they have suffered *before* our parents first sinned? This problem caused agonies of perplexity to the pious biologists of a hundred years ago.

Some forms of punishment here on earth are specially reserved for sinners. Persecutors of the early Church, as Lactantius pointed out, were apt to be eaten of worms. The death of Arius, who held shocking opinions on the Trinity, was a warning to sinners: his bowels gushed out, as did those of some less famous heretics. But Montaigne pointed out that the same fate had befallen men of undoubted virtue; it only remained, therefore, to fall back on the mysterious dispensations of Providence.

The favorite argument was, and perhaps still is, the argument from design. Could this universe, obedient as it is to natural laws, have come about without a Lawgiver? Could the sublimity of the starry heavens, the majesty of the ocean, the song of the skylark, and the loveliness of spring flowers, have come about by chance? As the poet sings:

Behold the snowflake exquisite in form,
Was it made perfect by unwilling norm?

The argument from design has, however, a logical
weakness when used by those who believe the Creator to be omnipotent. Design implies the necessity
of using means, which does not exist for omnipotence.
When we desire a house, we have to go through the
labor of building it, but Aladdin's genie could cause a
palace to exist by magic. The long process of evolution might be necessary to a divine Artificer who
found matter already in existence, and had to struggle
to bring order out of chaos. But to the God of Genesis
and of orthodox theology no such laborious process
was needed; no gradual process, no adaptation of
means to ends, was required by the Being who could
say: Let there be light, and there was light. The vast
astronomical and geological ages before life existed
may have been inevitable for a finite Deity working
in a reluctant material, but for Omnipotence they
would have been a gratuitous waste of time.

Let us then consider the hypothesis (which now has
influential advocates) of a God who is not omnipotent,
who is well meaning, but has constantly to struggle
against obstacles put in his way by pre-existing Nature.

This hypothesis, it must be said, cannot be dis-
proved. There is nothing known about the universe
that proves it to be false. But it is open to the same
objection that we formerly used against Leibniz, that
is to say, that a non-omnipotent devil is at least as
plausible as a non-omnipotent God. On this hypothesis, we shall suppose that the universe originally consisted only of matter, with the sole exception of Satan,
who studied it scientifically with a view to discovering

its potentialities of evil. He soon saw that there could be no evil without life, and he therefore set to work to discover how to create life. He had to wait a long time, till the nebula had condensed into stars, the stars had thrown out planets, and the planets had cooled. At last, when the moment had arrived so far as physics was concerned, he set to work to study chemistry, and discovered that a certain compound, if he could synthesize it, would be at once sentient and self-perpetuating. After many efforts, he succeeded in making the germ of life; then, with the sense of labor rewarded, he mumbled:

Mischief, thou are afoot! Now let it work.

At first the process was regrettably slow. Sea slime had only the rudiments of feeling, and even when evolution had got as far as oysters their pangs were still regrettably dim. But after that things began to go better. Sharks kept humbler fishes in a state of terror, hawks made little birds miserable, and cats brought tragedy into the lives of mice. But there was still something lacking: in between times, animals would persist in being happy, and forgetting the horrors that the next moment might bring. At last, to Satan's infinite delight, Man was evolved, with the fatal gifts of memory and foresight. Each horror that happened to Man left its indelible mark in his mind; he could not forget that what had occurred might occur again, and in warding off misfortune he lost the joy of life. Furious at his own misery, he sought the cause in the misdeeds of other men, and turned upon them in savage battle, thus magnifying a thousand times the ills that Nature has provided. With increasing glee, Satan watched the dismal process. At last, to crown his joy, men appeared who suffered not only from their own suffering, but from that of all mankind. Their preaching roused their followers to anger against those who refused to accept it, and so in the end increased the sum of human misery. When Satan saw this, his happiness was at last complete.

But all this is nothing but a pleasant fancy. Men, as is natural, have an intense desire to humanize the universe: God and Satan, alike, are essentially human figures, the one a projection of ourselves, the other of our enemies. Both alike have purposes, and their activities, like ours, spring from desire. A somewhat difficult effort of imagination is required before we can conceive a universe without purpose, developing blindly in accordance with aimless habits. We feel an impulse to ask why? meaning not from what causes, but to what end. The Greeks thought that the sun and moon and planets were each moved about by a god, who was actuated by an æsthetic love of regularity such as inspired the Parthenon. This view made the heavens feel cozy. But gradually it was discovered that the regularity is only approximate: the planets move in ellipses, not in circles, and even the ellipses are inaccurate. The only thing that seemed to remain precise and exact was Newton's law of gravitation, though now we know that this too was only roughly true. However, there certainly seemed to be laws of nature, and where there are laws (we are told) there must be a Lawgiver.

In the period immediately following Newton this point of view had much plausibility, and convinced even such temperamental skeptics as Voltaire. But alas! The laws of nature are not what they used to be; they have become mere statistical averages. There is no longer anything in physics to suggest the Almighty Watchmaker, who made such a superlative watch that it only had to be wound up once. The laws of nature, like the laws of chance, are only verified when large numbers of instances are concerned, and then only approximately. Moreover, the universe, like humanly made watches, and unlike the superlative watch of 18th Century theology, is running down; energy is only useful when it is unevenly distributed, and it is continually approaching nearer and nearer to complete equality of distribution. When once this perfection of cosmic democracy has been achieved, nothing of the slightest interest to man or God or devil can ever happen again, unless omnipotence sees fit to wind the watch up once more.

But after all, the champion of cosmic purpose will say, it is *Life* that exhibits the important part of the divine plan; the rest is only stage scenery. Before Darwin, the marvellous adaptation of animals to their environment was regarded as evidence of benevolent purpose on the part of the Deity, but the theory of natural selection provided a scientific explanation of a vast collection of facts which had been serviceable to the theologians. We can now see, in a general way, how, given the chemical properties of living substance, ordinary physical and chemical forces were likely to set the process of evolution in motion. True, we cannot manufacture life in the laboratory, and until we have done so it is open to the orthodox to maintain that we shall never be able to do so. But for my part I see no reason why organic chemists could not, within the next hundred years, manufacture living microorganisms. It may take some time—say a million years —to cause these to develop by artificial selection into giraffes and hippopotamuses and tigers. When this has been achieved, no doubt the theologians will still maintain that MAN can only be made by the Deity, but I fear the biologists will soon refute this last hope. Whether artificial man will be better or worse than the natural sort I do not venture to predict.

There would seem, therefore, to be no evidence that the course of events has been planned either by an omnipotent or by a non-omnipotent Deity; there is also no evidence that it has not been planned. Nor, if there be a Deity, is there any evidence as to his moral attributes. He may be doing His best under difficulties; He may be doing His worst, but be unable to prevent the accidental emergence of a little bit of good now and then. Or, again, His purposes may be purely æsthetic; He may not care whether His creatures are happy or unhappy, but only whether they provide a pleasing spectacle. All these hypotheses are equally probable, in the sense that there is not a shred of evidence for or against any of them. Nor should we neglect the Zoroastrian hypothesis of two Great Spirits, one good and one bad, the good one to achieve final victory when Persia conquers all the world. Aristotle thought there were 47 or 55 gods; this view also deserves our charitable respect. Of possible hypotheses there is no end, but in the absence of evidence we have no right to incline towards those that we happen to find agreeable.

What are we to think of immortality? To most modern Christians this question seems to be bound up with that of the existence of God, but both historically and logically the questions are quite distinct. Buddhists, though in their early days they were Atheists, believed that the soul survives death, except when such a pitch of virtue has been achieved as to deserve Nirvana. The Jews of the Old Testament, though they believed in God, did not (for the most part) believe in immortality. Clearly both these views are possible; the question of immortality is therefore, at least in some degree, distinct from that of the existence of God.

In the natural theology that has grown up in Christian civilizations, the two questions are connected through Divine Justice. The good, in this life, are not always happy, nor are the wicked always unhappy. Therefore, if the world is governed by a just God, there must be a future life, where the good will enjoy eternal bliss and the wicked will suffer eternal torment —or at any rate such purifying pains as may ultimately make them good. *If* there is a just God, and *if* there is free will (without which sin becomes meaningless), there is some force in this argument. Are there any others that should convince us of the immortality of the soul?

First of all, what is meant by "the soul"? We are supposed to consist of two things, one called a body, the other called the mind or soul. The body can be weighed on a weighing machine, it can move about, fall downstairs, have pieces cut off by a surgeon, and so on. The mind, meanwhile, does quite other things: it thinks and feels and wills. If my leg is amputated, no part of my soul is cut off; conversely, when I sleep my body remains intact. Among the movements of my body, we can distinguish those that spring from the mind from those that have a purely physical origin: if I walk along a street, I do so because my mind has so chosen, but if I slip on a piece of orange peel my mind has no part in causing the consequent collapse. These distinctions are so familiar that we take them as a matter of course, but their origin is in fact theological rather than scientific. They begin with Plato, so far as explicit philosophy is concerned, but were taken over by him from the Orphic religion. From Plato, and also from some other sources, the separation of soul and body was taken over by Christianity, and in time people came to think of it as an unquestionable truth.

But in fact both soul and body are metaphysical abstractions; what we know from experience are occurrences. We know thoughts, but not the supposed thinker; we know particular volitions, but not the will *per se*. Nor are we in any better case as regards the body. Physicists, who are supposed to know most about matter, say the oddest things about it. According to them, it is merely a convenient fiction; what really goes on in the physical world, they say, is a perpetual redistribution of energy, sometimes by sudden explosions, sometimes in gradually spreading waves. The body, which seems so solid and familiar, consists, they say, mainly of holes in waves of probability. If you do not understand what this means, I will confess that I do not either. But however that may be, it is clear that my body, which is described on my passport, and my mind, which is described by other philosophers, are alike mainly convenient ways of grouping phenomena, and that phenomena, so far as we know them, have not the characteristics that we associate either with mind or with body, since they are brief and evanescent. The phenomena, in fact, are not specially mental or specially material; they are the raw material out of which, for convenience of discourse, we construct the systems that we call minds and bodies.

The question of the immortality of the soul can, however, be restated so as to take account of these modern theories. Our thoughts and feelings, while we live, are linked together by memory and experience. We can inquire whether, after we are dead, there will still be thoughts and feelings that remember those we had when we lived on earth, for, if there will be, they may be regarded as still belonging to us, in the only sense in which our thoughts and feelings in this life belong to us.

Stated in this way, it must be said that immortality appears exceedingly improbable. Memory is clearly associated with the brain, and there is nothing to suggest that memory can survive after the brain has disintegrated. This seems as improbable as that a fire will survive after it has burnt everything combustible in its neighborhood. It would be going too far to say that we *know* such things to be impossible; we seldom know enough to say that this or that *cannot* happen. But on ordinary scientific grounds, seeing the intimate correlation of mental and cerebral organization, we can say that the survival of the one without the other must remain no more than a bare possibility, with much evidence against it and none in its favor.

But, even supposing the dogmas of religion to be false, it may be urged that they afford comfort to believers and do little harm. That they do little harm is not true. Opposition to birth control makes it impossible to solve the population problem, and therefore postpones indefinitely all chance of world peace; it also secures, wherever the law is what the Catholic vote has made it in Connecticut, that women incapable of surviving childbirth shall die in futile confinements. The influence of the Anglican Church in England suffices to insure that victims of cancer shall suffer agonies as long as possible, however much they themselves may desire euthanasia. Orthodox Protestantism in Tennessee suffices to prevent honest teaching of biology. Not only, however, where the law intervenes does orthodoxy do harm. I was myself at one time officially concerned in the appointment of a philosophy professor in an important American university; all the others agreed that of course he must be a good Christian. Practically all philosophers of any intellectual eminence are openly or secretly freethinkers; the insistence on orthodoxy therefore necessitated the appointment of a nonentity or a humbug.

On many important moral issues of modern times, the Church has thrown its influence on the side of cruelty or illegality. I will give two examples. Leopold, King of the Belgians, was also King of the Congo "Free" State. His rule involved what were probably the worst and most systematic atrocities in the long blood-stained annals of the oppression of Negroes by white men. When the facts became known, the Belgian Socialist Party, which consisted of free-thinkers, did everything in its power to mitigate the horrors of the King's personal tyranny; the Church, on the contrary, was obstructive and tried in every possible way to interfere with the publicity of those who were denouncing the horrors. The Church failed, but if the natives of the Belgian Congo no longer suffer as they did it is no thanks to the professed followers of Christ who occupied the important posts in the Catholic hierarchy.

The other example is more recent. It is supposed that we are fighting to secure the reign of law and the victory of democracy. Spain had a legally elected democratic government, but the Church disliked it. Pious Generals who were orthodox sons of the Church made a military insurrection against the legal and democratic government, and in the end the Church, with the help of Hitler and Mussolini, was successful in reimposing tyranny on the gallant Spanish champions of freedom. In this contest America officially refused to lift a finger to help the Loyalists, and even strained the interpretation of the law so as to prevent help from being given to the Loyalists by private American citizens. The government took this line in order to please American Catholics, with the result, not only that the Spaniards suffer, but that we have lost a possible ally in the war. The British government, perhaps for somewhat different reasons, was at least equally culpable.

Christian orthodoxy, however, is no longer the chief danger to free thought. The greatest danger in our day comes from new religions, Communism and Nazism. To call these religions may perhaps be objectionable both to their friends and to their enemies, but in fact they have all the characteristics of religions. They advocate a way of life on the basis of irrational dogmas; they have a sacred history, a Messiah, and a priesthood. I do not see what more could be demanded to qualify a doctrine as a religion. But let us examine each of them a little more narrowly.

When I speak of communism in this connection, I do not mean the doctrine that men's goods ought to be held in common. This is an ancient doctrine, advocated by Plato, apparently held by the primitive Church, revived constantly by religious sects during the middle ages, and condemned by one of the 39 Articles of the Church of England. With its truth or falsehood I am not concerned; what I am concerned with is the doctrine of the modern Communistic Party, and of the Russian Government to which it owes allegiance.

According to this doctrine, the world develops on the lines of a Plan called Dialectical Materialism, first discovered by Karl Marx, embodied in the practice of a great state by Lenin, and now expounded from day to day by a Church of which Stalin is the Pope. Those who disagree with the Pope either as to doctrine or as to church government are to be liquidated if possible; if that is not possible, they are to be bamboozled. Free discussion is to be prevented wherever the power to do so exists; revelation is to be interpreted, without argument, not by democratic process, but by the dicta of ecclesiastical dignitaries. It has already become apparent that the original ethic of the early communists, like that of the early Christians, while still treated with verbal respect, is not to be followed in actual life; indeed those who would *practise* communism, like the Franciscans who practised apostolic poverty, are heretics, to be suppressed with the utmost rigor of persecution. If this doctrine and this organization prevail, free inquiry will become as impossible as it was in the middle ages, and the world will relapse into bigotry and obscurantism.

The theory of the Nazis, however, is definitely worse. Let us consider its salient points. There is a master race, the Germans, which is divinely ordained to rule the rest of mankind, not for their good, but for its own. Originally it was thought that races akin to the Germans shared some of their merits, but this turned out to be a mistake; in Norway, for instance, there are no genuine Nordics except Quisling and a handful of followers. Non-Aryans are specially wicked, and the most wicked of non-Aryans are the Jews. The Japanese, on the other hand, are so virtuous that they may count as honorary Aryans.

The Germans, alas, have been corrupted by Jewish influences, notably Christ and Marx. What they were before this unfortunate poison got into their blood may be seen in the pages of Tacitus. When it has been eliminated, they will again perceive that war is the noblest of human activities, and the opportunity of tyranny its most splendid reward. Other nations, strange to say, seem blind to the superiority of the Germans, but it was hoped that tanks and planes would prove efficient missionaries of the new creed. This hope, however, is now rapidly fading.

No such tissue of nonsense could have been believed by any population trained to examine evidence scientifically, and to base its opinions on rational grounds. Self-esteem, personal, national, or human, is one of the great sources of irrational belief; in the case of the Nazis, the self-esteem is national. Education should be directed, in part, to teaching the young to think independently of their prejudices, especially their collective prejudices, which are politically the most harmful. But this is not done anywhere; every national government finds national self-esteem useful, every rich government finds admiration of the plutocracy useful, every obscurantist government finds credulity useful. Nowhere, therefore, except among the esoteric elite of a few universities, is anything done to promote an honest attempt to decide questions according to the evidence. And so credulous populations are left defenseless against the wiles of clever politicians, who

lead them through inflated self-esteem to hatred, from
hatred to war, from war to universal misery. The modern advances in the art of propaganda have been met
with no corresponding advances in training to resist
propaganda. And so the populations of the world, one
by one as "civilization" reaches them, go down into a
dark pit of madness, where all that is worth preserving
perishes in aimless slaughter.

The creed that I am preaching, if it can be called a
creed, is a simple one: that, if you have an opinion
about any matter, it should be based on ascertained
facts, not upon hope or fear or prejudice. There is a
known educational technique by which pupils of average intelligence can be taught to discount their passions when they think, but almost everywhere the authorities prevent the use of this technique. The authorities, almost everywhere, are convinced that they
would be overthrown if the public were to examine
their claims dispassionately; they therefore encourage
passionate as opposed to rational thinking. Sooner or
later, they become so tyrannical that they are overthrown, passionately, not rationally. After the pot of
passion has boiled long enough, a new crust forms,
and the new authorities are usually no better than the
old. Louis XVI is executed, and is succeeded, first by
Robespierre, then by Napoleon. Tsar Nicholas is as-
sassinated, and a stricter tyranny follows under Lenin
and Stalin. To this rule the American Revolution is
one of the rare exceptions, and it was led by freethinkers; Washington and Adams, just as much as Jefferson, rejected the orthodoxy that most of their followers accepted.

Few modern obscurantists have the courage to say

that it is better to believe what is false than what is true. In antiquity and in the 17th and 18th centuries it was commonly held that religion was necessary to keep the poor submissive, and should therefore be believed by them although aristocrats might have seen through it. Even in the 19th century, many French freethinkers liked their wives to be believers, in the hope that it would keep them chaste. But democracy and votes for women have made these points of view obsolete; now-a-days, if you wish to advocate religion for the masses, you must advocate it for everyone, and if you are to advocate it for everyone you must do so, at least nominally, on the ground that you believe it to be true.

The insincerity of this appeal to truth is shown by the unwillingness to trust to free discussion or to allow the scientific habit of mind to be taught in education. If you think that a doctrine can only be rendered acceptable by the stake or the concentration camp, you evidently have not much confidence in the rational grounds in its favor. If you think it is necessary to forbid the publication or sale of books which contradict your opinions, you evidently hold that such books, in a free intellectual competition, would be likely to get the best of the argument.

You may, of course, fall back on an anti-democratic point of view. You may say: We, the Censors, or we the dignitaries of the Church, or we the agents for government propaganda, are wise men and trained investigators; we have examined all the evidence, and reached a conclusion, which happens, by a mere coincidence, to be in line with the interest of the authorities. But the populace have not the time to study such questions deeply; subversive agitators will, if we leave them free, make appeals to vulgar passions, which it would require much time and work to combat. Since we know the truth, is it not better that we should impart it, and should forbid all attempts to cause the dissemination of what our wisdom shows to be falsehood? Let us teach humility to the public, and then tell them from time to time what we deem it good that they should know. In this way all the time spent on futile and vexatious argumentation will be saved.

Where the truth really is known, there is something to be said for this view. The multiplication table is taught dogmatically; a teacher who held heretical opinions about it would hardly get a job. But in such matters there is no need of censorship; no one in fact holds heretical views about the multiplication table. Heretical views arise when the truth is uncertain, and it is only when the truth is uncertain that censorship is invoked. In fact, it is difficult to find anything really certain outside the realm of pure mathematics and some facts of history and geography. If suppression of free discussion is necessary in order to cause an opinion to be believed, that in itself is evidence that the rational grounds in favor of the opinion are inadequate, for if they were adequate free discussion would be the best way of making the opinion prevail. When the authorities profess to *know* something which to the unprejudiced person seems doubtful or false, they are either themselves the victims of prejudice, or they are dishonestly trying to represent the interest of their class or creed or nation as coinciding with the general interest. In either case, interference with free discussion can only do harm.

Some one may object that, while free thought may be all very well in the abstract, it won't do in this actual world, because fanaticism is needed for victory in battle. Other things being equal, we may be told, the holders of an irrational warlike creed will always win the victory over peaceful folk who only want a quiet life. There is no doubt an element of truth in this argument, but it is a small element, and what truth it contains is only for the short run. The Germans and Japanese, by means of their fanaticism, were able to win initial victories; but their very fanaticism roused the hostility of the world, and is leading to their downfall. Fanatics, just because they lack the scientific temper, cannot weigh risks calmly, and are prone to overestimate the chances of victory. In the long run, fanaticism is incompatible with scientific excellence, which is the most important source of strength in modern war. In a war between a scientific and a fanatical nation, given equal material resources, the scientific nation is pretty sure to be victorious.

We have wandered into political and social questions, but the core of the argument for free thought lies in the individual life. It is good to ask ourselves, from time to time, what sort of person we should wish to be. When I ask myself this question, I find that I desire at once a kind of pride and a kind of humility. As for pride: I do not wish to be forced or cajoled into any opinion because others desire that I should hold it, nor do I wish to be the victim of my own hopes and fears to the extent of allowing myself to live in an unreal world of pleasant make-believe. I respect, in myself and others, the power of thought and of scientific investigation, by means of which we have acquired whatever knowledge we possess of the universe in which we live. And thought, when it is genuine thought, has its own intrinsic morality and its own brand of asceticism. But it has also its rewards: a happiness, amounting at moments to ecstasy, in understanding what had been obscure, and surveying in a unified vision what had seemed detached and chaotic fragments.

But the pursuit of truth, when it is profound and genuine, requires also a kind of humility which has some affinity to submission to the will of God. The universe is what it is, not what I choose that it should be. If it is indifferent to human desires, as it seems to be; if human life is a passing episode, hardly noticeable in the vastness of cosmic processes; if there is no superhuman purpose, and no hope of ultimate salvation, it is better to know and acknowledge this truth than to endeavor, in futile self-assertion, to order the universe to be what we find comfortable.

Towards facts, submission is the only rational attitude, but in the realm of ideals there is nothing to which to submit. The universe is neither hostile nor friendly; it neither favors our ideals nor refutes them. Our individual life is brief, and perhaps the whole life of mankind will be brief if measured on an astronomical scale. But that is no reason for not living it as seems best to us. The things that seem to us good are none the less good for not being eternal, and we should not ask of the universe an external approval of our own ethical standards.

The freethinker's universe may seem bleak and cold to those who have been accustomed to the comfortable indoor warmth of the Christian cosmology. But to those who have grown accustomed to it, it has its own sublimity, and confers its own joys. In learning to think freely we have learnt to thrust fear out of our thoughts, and this lesson, once learnt, brings a kind of peace which is impossible to the slave of hesitant and uncertain credulity.

Mentalism vs. Materialism

Ever since Greek times there has been a controversy between those who regarded matter and those who regarded mind as the dominant power in the universe. Religious orthodoxy, whether pagan or Christian, has always tended to be associated with the Mentalist party. The Materialist party, on the other hand, has tended to ally itself with scientific orthodoxy. This alliance has sometimes been too intimate for prudence, for when new discoveries required a change in scientific doctrine, the older formulations of Materialism were apt to become untenable, thus enabling the Mentalists to claim that the latest results of science favored their case. This familiar process has been repeated in recent years; quantum theory, in particular, has been interpreted by theologically orthodox commentators as involving the bankruptcy of Materialism. For my part, I think this interpretation, in the main, mistaken. It is true that it would be better to substitute the word "physicalism" for the word "materialism": I should define "physicalism" as the doctrine that events are governed by the laws of physics. But this change has no theological implications whatever. It does not make it any more probable that the world has a purpose, or that it is evolving towards better things, or that it has any other property that would be agreeable to our cosmic hopes.

THE MEANING OF MATTER

"Matter," as formerly understood, was a straightforward common-sense concept, derived from the concept "thing"; it meant whatever occupied space, and displayed its existence by the qualities of hardness, resistance, and impenetrability. The atomists, in particular, thought of the world as composed of tiny billiard balls perpetually bumping into each other. This was a picture that anybody could imaginatively understand, and if it had been scientifically adequate physics would have been a very easy science. But a number of discoveries, mostly made within the last half-century, have shown that this simple picture will not do.

THE NATURE OF "MASS"

"Mass" used to be defined as "quantity of matter," but it was found that the mass of a body in rapid motion is greater than that of the same body at rest; if a body could move with the velocity of light its mass would become infinite. Since motion is relative the mass of a body will be differently estimated by different observers, according to their motion relative to the body. Thus mass is not an intrinsic property of a body, but is dependent on its relation to the observer who measures the mass. The result has been that mass has come to be viewed as a form of energy; the mass of a body is diminished when it emits energy, and increased when it absorbs energy.

This is not a mere theory, or a question of trivial

correction; it is held that the sun, which is continually radiating energy in the form of light and heat, is losing mass at the rate of four million tons per second. All the other stars are doing likewise, at varying rates, according to their size and temperature. This mass is transformed into other kinds of energy, but these, for the most part, are not associated with what common sense would call "things." The stars, like a morning mist, are gradually dissolving into invisibility; in the end there will be only heat. On this ground alone we can no longer attribute to matter the comfortable solidity that it used to enjoy.

UPS AND DOWNS OF THE ATOMIC THEORY

The ups and downs of the atomic theory have been interesting. For a long time there were supposed to be 92 "elements," each having its own sort of atom. Then the picture was simplified: it appeared that each atom could be regarded as a system composed of only two kinds of constituents, electrons and protons. The electron had a negative charge of electricity, the proton an equal positive charge; the proton had about 1,850 times the mass of an electron. An atom consisted of a nucleus (composed of a number of protons and a small number of electrons) and a number of planetary electrons just sufficient to make the total number of electrons equal to the total number of protons. This was called, after its inventors, the Rutherford-Bohr atom.

This atom had for a while a great success, as it explained many observed facts almost perfectly. But after a reign of 12 years (1913-1925) it was deposed in favor of the Heisenberg-Schrodinger atom, which was a much more abstract and less imaginable affair. It is still permissible to talk about electrons and protons, just as we talk of sunrises and sunsets in spite of Copernicus; but the ultimate truth is supposed to be something different. Even on the level on which we can still retain electrons and protons two new kinds of units have to be added, called neutrons and positrons. The neutron is like the proton, except that it is not electrified; the positron is like the electron, except that its electricity is positive instead of negative. Perhaps the proton consists of a neutron and a positron, but this is uncertain. If this view proves tenable matter may be regarded, for most practical purposes, as composed of three kinds of fundamental units, neutrons, positrons, and electrons. But this is to be taken as no more than an approximation, permitted as a concession to our desire for an imaginative picture of physical processes.

QUANTUM THEORY

What really happens, according to quantum theory, can only be expressed in mathematical symbols, and even then not accurately; there is a theoretical limit to the accuracy with which the state of a material system can be ascertained. It is impossible to make modern quantum theory simple, but I will try to state, in general terms, what is relevant to our topic.

An atom, according to this theory, is a small region within which there is a certain amount of energy—an amount which is not constant, but changes discontinuously from one to another of certain possible values that are separated from each other by finite amounts.

The amount of energy in the atom is increased when energy is absorbed from without and diminished when energy is emitted in the form of radiation. It is only when atoms emit energy that they have the kind of effects by which our senses are affected; a collection of atoms that all retained their energy would emit no light, and therefore be invisible. It is therefore only *changes* of energy that afford material for observation; what goes on in the atom while the energy within it remains unchanged is a matter of guesswork, as to which, from the very nature of the case, evidence is impossible.

THE BEHAVIOR OF MATTER IN BULK

There are rules governing the changes that atoms undergo from one energy-level to another, but these rules are not sufficient to determine which of several possible things an individual atom will do. They do, however, suffice to determine the average behavior of a large number of atoms. The case is analogous to throwing dice: with two dice there are 36 possibilities, and if the dice are "true" each of the 36 possibilities will be realized about equally often in a very large number of throws. So it is with atoms: given a very great many atoms, all capable of a certain definite set of transitions, we can tell, almost exactly, what proportion will choose each possibility, though we cannot tell which will be chosen by any one particular atom. Consequently the behavior of matter in bulk is statistically deterministic, although each separate atom may make any one of a certain definite set of transitions.

It will be seen that in this theory "matter" has been completely absorbed into "energy." An atom is merely a small region in which is concentrated a certain amount of energy, which is not constant, but undergoes variations which are subject to certain rules. There is nothing that can be called "substantial identity" between an atom at one time and what at another time we choose to regard as the "same" atom.

PHYSICS IS STILL DETERMINISTIC

The failure of determinism, where atomic occurrences are concerned, has much less importance than is sometimes attributed to it. Except in a well-equipped physical laboratory nothing can be discovered about the behavior of an individual atom or electron; all the occurrences of which we are aware in ordinary life involve many millions of atoms, and are therefore just as predictable as they used to be. It is true that the prediction is now only probable, but the probability is so near to certainty that the element of doubt due to this cause is very much less than that which will always be present owing to other causes. Dependence upon statistical regularity occurs also within classical physics. It might happen, for example, that all the air in a room would collect itself in one half of the room, leaving a vacuum in the other half. We cannot say that this is impossible, but it is so improbable that a rational man would disbelieve the statement that it had happened on a certain occasion, even if the statement were made by all the Fellows of the Royal Society together with the Archbishops of Canterbury and York. For practical purposes, therefore, physics is still deterministic; the only change is that the deterministic laws are all statistical.

What, assuming the truth of modern physics, can

we know about the physical world? There is no longer
reason to believe that there is such a thing as "matter"
consisting of atoms that persist and move. There is
a collection of events ordered in the four-dimensional
manifold of space-time. There is something called "energy," of which the total amount is constant, but of
which the distribution is continually changing; moreover, energy has many different forms. Some of these
forms characterize regions in which, for common sense,
there is matter; others, like light, do not. We know
something of the rules governing the changes in the
distribution of energy, and its transitions from one
form into another. It seems that these rules are sufficient to determine large-scale phenomena with a degree of accuracy and certainty which suffices for practical purposes, but the small-scale occurrences within
the region that we call a single atom are not determined except to this extent, that in given circumstances
what will happen must be one of certain enumerable
possibilities, and the probability of each of these possibilities is determined by physical laws.

PSYCHOLOGY ALSO HAS CHANGED

Let us now turn to psychology, which, though a
much less developed science than physics, has nevertheless gone through some not wholly dissimilar
changes. In medieval and Cartesian orthodoxy there
were two kinds of substance, mental and material; the
business of material substance was to occupy space,
and the business of mental substance was to "think."
In modern physics, "substance" has disappeared: instead of persistent "things" that occupy space we have
brief events that occupy space-time. In psychology,

similarly, "substance" has disappeared. Descartes, after arguing "I think, therefore I am," goes on to say: "I am a thing that thinks." In the modern view "I" is a merely grammatical term; all that we know about thoughts can, if we choose, be expressed without the use of this word. Personal identity, like the identity of a piece of matter, is not the persistence of a "thing," but a certain kind of causal connection between a series of events. In psychology the causal connection of most importance in defining personal identity is memory.

LIFE AS IT APPEARS IN BIOLOGY

Ignoring for the moment the question of "thought," let us first view life as it appears in biology. There is increasing reason to think that the whole of the difference between living and dead matter is chemical: living matter has the capacity of transforming suitable other matter into something of the same chemical composition as itself. Plants can do this with inorganic matter, animals (broadly speaking) only with organic matter. The whole process of the transformation of soil into grain and grain into human bodies, though very complicated, is essentially of the same nature as the transformation of hydrogen and oxygen into water. There is no reason why it should not be possible, before very long, to generate living organisms in the laboratory. And it is clear that a chemical compound having the above characteristic of assimilation is bound, given opportunity, to spread in the kind of way in which living matter has spread.

From the standpoint of psychology the most important property of living matter is habit-formation. This property is not *wholly* absent in dead matter: paper which has been in a roll will roll itself up again if you flatten it out. But examples of habit in inorganic matter are few and unimportant. In living matter they are still rare among the lowest forms of life; they are more noteworthy among mammals than among other animals, and much more noteworthy among human beings than among the highest apes. A great deal of what we call "intelligence" consists in aptitude for the formation of useful habits; it includes, for example, skill in games, quickness in learning the multiplication table, and facility in acquiring languages. I do not contend that the acquisition of habits covers the *whole* of what we mean by intellectual or artistic ability; I say only that it covers much of the ground, and that it covers a good deal more than might appear at first sight. It certainly covers at least nine-tenths of what is tested in examinations.

WHAT WE MEAN BY HABIT

What, exactly, do we mean by habit? Let us take the matter first as it appears to external observation, in the behavior of animal bodies. An animal has certain ways of responding to stimuli that are independent of its experience—withdrawal from what is painful, approach to food that looks or smells good, and also certain specific reflexes such as sneezing, yawning, and making the noises characteristic of the species. Sucking in infancy and sexual behavior in adult life come under the same head. Now it is found that, if a kind of event A often happens to an animal at the same time as another kind of event B, and if B produces a reaction C, then in time A without B will produce the reaction C. When my puppy infringes the moral law I chastise it, and at the same time say "bad dog" in a tone of reprobation. The puppy slinks away to escape the chastisement, but in time it learns to slink away when I utter a reproof. A dog that enjoys a walk learns to jump and bark excitedly as soon as his master puts on a great-coat. All training of domestic animals proceeds on this principle.

Knowing a language, whether one's own or another, is entirely a matter of habit-formation. If someone shouts "Fire!" you feel the same kind of emotion as if you saw the fire, and behave in a similar way. Obscene literature is forbidden because it arouses, though more faintly, the passions that would be aroused by what it describes. The words "William the Conqueror, 1066," become a verbal habit during early years at school; a sufficient number of such habits will make you a learned historian. Memory is one kind of habit. All learning by experience consists in the formation of habits, in accordance with the proverb "once bit, twice shy."

HABIT PRIMARILY PHYSICAL

From our point of view, the important thing about habit is that it is primarily physiological rather than psychological. Consequently the psychological area covered by it is brought into subjection to a kind of causation that is physical rather than mental, and the greater the region of habit the wider is the range of mental phenomena deprived of causal autonomy. The causal framework of the laws of human behavior seems to be, at any rate in the main, a matter, not for psychology, but for physics, chemistry, and physiology. I say "in the main" because the question is one to be decided by surveying the field in detail, not by any general principle assumed in advance of investigations.

It remains to examine a concept which is held to be peculiar to mental occurrences, namely "introspection."

The traditional view is that there are two kinds of senses, the "outer senses" and the "inner sense." The outer senses are supposed to tell us what goes on in the physical world, while the inner sense tells us what goes on in our own mind. The outer senses tell me that my friend So-and-so is coming along the street, while the inner sense tells me that I am glad to see him. "Introspection" consists of knowing occurrences by means of the inner sense; it is supposed to show us that there are in the world thoughts and feelings as well as events in space.

This way of looking at things seems to me radically mistaken; I do not believe there is any such duality of inner and outer senses. I hold that everything directly known by the senses happens in me, not in the outer world. I might say, roughly, that I believe only in the inner sense, but this would be somewhat misleading. What I can say is that the senses directly reveal thoughts and feelings and sensations, while events in the outer world have to be inferred.

As regards what would traditionally be called the outer senses, this point of view is forced on us by the physical causation of our sensations. When I have the experience which we call "seeing the sun" the immediate causal antecedents of my experience are in the eye, the optic nerve, and the brain. If my eye were subjected to the same physical stimulus as it normally receives from the light of the sun (which is obviously possible, at least in theory), I should have exactly the experience which is called "seeing the sun." Consequently it cannot be said that in this experience I am aware of the sun itself, since I can have the experience without the sun being present. We can go farther: if a surgeon could directly stimulate the optic nerve as it is usually stimulated by sunlight falling on the eye, I should still have an experience indistinguishable from "seeing the sun"; and so I should if it were the appropriate center in the brain that was stimulated, not the optic nerve. Therefore all that is certainly involved when I think I see the sun is my own sensation and an occurrence in my brain. And the occurrence in the brain is known only by a long and difficult process of scientific inference; what I know directly is only my own sensation.

PHYSICAL CAUSES OF INTROSPECTION

According to this view, the outer senses, such as those of sight and hearing and touch, are much more akin to what is commonly called introspection than is usually supposed. Does there, then, remain any valid distinction more or less corresponding to the old distinction of inner and outer senses? I think there does. When I see the sun other people can see it too; when I listen to a politician making a speech other people in the same hall can also hear him. This leads us to infer a common outside cause for the similar visual or auditory sensations of different people in the same environment. But when I feel a toothache others in the same room with me usually feel nothing similar. We conclude that the toothache is private, while the sun and the speech are public. The toothache, like seeing the sun and hearing the speech, has a physical cause, but the cause is in my body and therefore does not affect other people as it affects me. I think, accordingly, that "introspection" may be defined as consisting of sensations whose physical causes are in my body and under my skin.

"But," you may object, "introspection is not concerned with such things as toothaches; it is concerned with thoughts and feelings. I may think that not all continuous functions can be differentiated, and I may be aware of thinking this; I may feel sorrow that Roosevelt is dead, and be aware of feeling this. It is knowledge of this sort that introspection reveals." I do not for a moment deny that there is knowledge of this sort; what I do deny is that it is fundamentally different from the knowledge directly obtained through the outer senses. As soon as we realize that the sun itself has only a remote causal connection with the experience called "seeing the sun," it becomes clear that this experience is not nearly so different as it seemed from thoughts and feelings. Whether we are aware of a sensation or whether we are aware of a thought, it is something happening to ourselves of which we are aware; we are never aware without interference of anything except events happening to ourselves. I refrain from attempting to define the word "aware," which I have been using. I have discussed the definition of this word elsewhere (cf. *Inquiry Into Meaning and Truth*), and as it is complicated and not very relevant I shall leave this question on one side.

THE PHYSICAL AND MENTAL OVERLAP

Discussions of mind and matter and their relations seldom trouble to give definitions of the terms involved; it seems to be thought that we all know by the light of nature that every person has a mind and a body, which are separate things. This point of view is not primitive, but was originally adopted for religious reasons. From Orphism it got into philosophy through Plato; Christian theology gave it the definiteness and sharpness of distinction which has now come to seem a matter of course to most people. I hold, on the contrary, that the distinction is by no means sharp, and that there are events which are both mental and physical. Let us try to obtain definitions of the adjectives "mental" and "physical," which, in our view of rejection of "substance," we must substitute for the substantives "mind" and "matter." If, as I have been contending, the world consists of events, we have to inquire whether there are characteristics by which some events can be classed as "physical" and some as "mental," and whether, if so, the two classes overlap.

DEFINITION OF "PHYSICAL"

Let us begin with the adjective "physical." My own definition of this adjective is one which may, at first sight, seem an odd one: I should define an event as "physical" when it is the sort of event that is dealt with by physics. Now the character of these events is only determined in certain very abstract respects: they have spatio-temporal positions, and they consist of changes in the distribution of something called "energy." True, there is one other characteristic of "physical" events which is essential, and that is their relation to sensations. Physics is an empirical science—that is to say, its laws are accepted because they are confirmed by observation. But here we meet with a difficulty: the physical world, as it appears in quantum theory, is quite unlike the world of our everyday perceptions, and it is not obvious how it can predict what our perceptions will be. The truth is that the empirical verification of physical laws depends upon something which is not properly a part of physics—namely, upon the correlation of physical events with sensations. When radiant energy of a certain frequency reaches the eye we see a certain color; if theory has predicted that frequency, our seeing of the corresponding color is held to be an empirical confirmation of the theory, but it only is a confirmation if the correlation of physical events with sensations is included, along with pure physics, as part of the total of theory to be verified.

Now sensations and perceptions are part of the subject-matter of psychology, and are commonly classed as "mental." Thus physics derives its empirical justification entirely from its connection with events belonging to the domain of psychology, which alone are capable of being data. "Data," as I intend the word, are to be defined as events known otherwise than by inference. All such events belong to psychology. I should define a "mental" event as one that can be known to some one otherwise than by inference—*i.e.*, as one that is or may be a "datum." By means of certain postulates—causality, induction, and spatio-temporal continuity—we can, from data, infer events which are not data. If you put an egg in boiling water and leave it, and when you return you find that it is boiled, you assume that it existed meanwhile. The egg that existed meanwhile was not something oval and whitish, such as you can see, but was a system of many billions of transitions of an unknown something from one energy-level to another; this is the egg of physics, whereas the egg that you see is the egg of psychology. It is because of your experience of the egg of psychology, which you can see and taste, that you believe in the effect of the boiling water of physics upon the egg of physics.

The egg of psychology cannot be supposed to exist in the absence of a percipient, since it is caused by the effect of our sense-organs upon energy that travels into their neighborhood. But although it exists only when it is perceived, it supplies our only reason for believing in the physical egg which can exist unseen.

THE RELATIONS BETWEEN MENTAL AND PHYSICAL EVENTS

The question of the relations between mental and physical events is complicated by the fact that, while mental events come first in the order of knowledge, physical events seem to be supreme in the region of causal efficiency. I repeat that I mean by "mental" events the kind of events that someone can perceive, and by "physical" events the sort of events that are dealt with in physics.

The knowledge conferred by physics is abstract and mathematical; it does not tell us anything about the intrinsic character of physical events. Physics does not entitle us to say that physical events differ from thoughts and feelings, nor yet that they do not differ. The inference to physical events is entirely by means of causal laws, which only enable us to infer structure. Let us take an illustration. A gramophone record can (with certain adjuncts) cause a piece of music; it can do so because of a certain identity of structure between the record and the music. But this identity is abstract and logical; in other respects the record is quite unlike the music. The physical causes of our sensations, in like manner, must have a certain structural similarity to the pattern of sensations that they cause, but need not otherwise resemble our sensations. If you could never perceive the record, and knew nothing about it except that it could cause the music, you would be in the same position with regard to it as you are with regard to the world of physics.

What physics treats as one event may, for aught that physics has to say to the contrary, be really a group of events, all in one spatio-temporal region. If what is for physics a bit of my brain is really a group of events, my sensations and thoughts and feelings may be members of this group. If so, the difference between the physical and the mental will be one of logical level: the unit for physics will be an assemblage of the units for psychology.

THE QUESTION OF "MATERIALISM"

The question of "materialism," as understood in the past, depended upon the notion of "substance"; in this old sense no one who rejects "substance" can be a Materialist. Nor can we be Materialists in the sense of believing that there are no mental events; mental events are more certain than physical events, since the physical is inferred from the mental by inferences, which confer only probability upon their conclusions.

But there is still a sense in which something closely akin to Materialism *may* be true, though it would be rash to say that it *is*. This sense has to do with the causal supremacy of physics. There is no reason whatever to suppose that living matter obeys laws different from those obeyed by dead matter. Although atomic physics is no longer deterministic, the physics of bodies of appreciable size remains as deterministic as it used to be. If there is a correlation between the state of the brain and the state of the mind, as it is plausible to suppose, then the laws of physics, together with the laws of this correlation, suffice to determine states of mind, unless (what seems improbable) the correlation is with a few atoms, not with larger portions of the brain. There is therefore some reason—though by no means conclusive reason—for regarding the laws of physics as, in a sense, controlling our mental life. This is a large part of what Materialists have contended, and this part of their contention *may* be true.